What Clinicians Are Saying

This amazing little book offers essential tools to transform our approach to therapy. I have always believed that symptoms are evidence of deeper distress and are therefore not sufficient targets for therapy; however too many modern approaches to therapy are technique-based and only scratch the surface. It is truly painful to see clients lose previous gains when symptoms reappear in yet another form. The wisdom shared here by Debra Littrell offers us a remedy to this impasse and challenges us to understand our clients in a deeper and more holistic way. By working collaboratively and experientially, we can guide clients through the preparation that is necessary to truly engage in healing work. I have found her materials to be invaluable in my clinical practice and am thrilled that she has chosen to share her insights with a broader audience. Brilliant!

Jackie G. Szarka, MA, PhD

Seattle, WA

I have been in Debra's consultation group for Eye Movement Desensitization and Reprocessing (EMDR Therapy) and have had the opportunity to learn a few of the somatic and energetic skills described in her book. These skills are simple and powerful tools to help individuals feel grounded and empowered by being more authentic. In helping my clients with these skills, I have found it useful to incorporate these skills as part of my own self care. Because of how clearly Debra has laid out the skills, transcripts of interactions and rationale for each, it is not necessary to have the training to effectively utilize the steps in her book. However, her book makes you want to learn more, and I look forward to continued learning in this area.

Beth Murphy, Psy.D.
Bellevue, WA

Somatic & Energetic Resourcing
Facilitating Clients Living Authentically

Somatic & Energetic
Facilitating Clients Living Authentically
Resourcing

A Practitioner's Guide
Debra A. Littrell

Transformation Media Books

Bloomington, IN

Copyright © 2015 Debra A. Littrell

Somatic & Energetic Resourcing™
Facilitating Clients Living Authentically

All rights reserved. No part of this book may be reproduced or transmitted in any form or by any means, electronic or mechanical, including photocopying, recording, or by any information storage and retrieval system, without permission in writing from the publisher.

Published by Transformation Media Books, USA

www.transformationmediabooks.com
An imprint of Pen & Publish, Inc.
Bloomington, Indiana
(812) 837-9226
info@PenandPublish.com
www.PenandPublish.com

Print ISBN-13: 978-1-941799-03-1
eBook ISBN: 978-1-941799-04-8

Co-editors: Kathy Smith, MC
May Johnstone, Ph.D.
Katy Murray, MSW, LICSW, BCD

Cover Concept: Debra Littrell
Cover Design: Mark Atteberry
Print Conversion: Islam Farid

The author and publisher of this book do not make any claim to or guarantee of results from the activities in this book. This book is not a substitute for training, consultation or psychotherapy. Results may vary depending on the individual employing and receiving the activities. If you or your client have a trauma or neglect history it is recommended you use the activities with a trained professional.

Dedication

This book is dedicated to all of you who have the courage and tenacity to give up your ego/personality/false self. To give up looking externally for your definition of self and how to live. Who have the courage to give up expecting others to change, and looking to others for change in yourself. Who have the courage and tenacity to discover Truth, and live, Authentically. Even if everyone else thinks you are nuts. Living Authentically™, the most powerful change agent there is!

Foreword

This work by Debra Littrell is so much needed in our world today. Have we ever been as disconnected from Self as we are now? More suffering believed to be related to mental health is occurring today, even by those who appear to be leading rather "successful" lives, from the point of view of the outside observer. Therein lies the issue – it is not what we appear to be from the outside that fulfills us. To be content we must learn to listen to our inner wisdom. We all possess this.

The very term *content* is not flashy and exciting, however. Therefore many of us resist contentment as a goal. It is not quite *good enough*. Holding the negative self-belief that we are *not good enough* affects every aspect of life, and tends to leave us feeling "less than" and out of control of our condition of being. As long as our definition of worth and joy is weighted more heavily in an outside image, and in what others judge as being worthwhile, there will be little joy and worth inside of ourselves.

I am a licensed clinical psychologist and have consulted with and come to be friends with Debra Littrell over the past six years. Her work and guidance have informed my practice quite profoundly. Many of my clients are dealing with traumatic pasts, and are not ready to jump right into the work of processing what continues to trigger them. Some clients are aware of symptoms, but not the causes.

Prior to learning Somatic & Energetic Resourcing, I had used several therapeutic tools to help clients calm the mind, body and emotions. Some such techniques included progressive muscle relaxation, and breathing, and visualization-relaxation exercises. Some clients were unable to become ready to do the work they truly needed with these tools. Once I began incorporating Somatic & Energetic Resourcing into my practice, energetic doors began to open up for my clients in new ways, and the activities helped them get in touch with what was true for them more fully. This Self Awareness is *essential* for greater congruence in life to flourish. A huge part of why I believe this worked well with my clients was because of my own growth as a person and clinician in deepening my Self Awareness.

Getting comfortable with being acutely aware is something that I had managed to squash throughout the years, as it "got in the way"; or so I had thought. I had worked in a very linear job as a neuropsychometrist, in which it is important to administer tests exactly as they are intended. This keeps any errors due to natural human variance within the acceptable margins. Otherwise, the information the test yields (scope of damage, i.e.: after a stroke) may not be accurate or helpful to the test taker. I did not know, at that time in my life, how to balance my internal and external responses as well as I have since learned. Thus, I had gotten out of the habit of listening to my internal responses in order to feel balanced as a test administrator.

Once I got into my clinical psychology program and learned that my intuition and sense of Self Awareness were not only useful, but *essential* in order to be of any help to others, I began to feel a healing take place. However, the totality of graduate school and the rest of life at the same time didn't allow for full awareness to always be with me. Working with

Foreword

Debra rounded this out for me, and I am so thankful to have come back to this most natural and true state.

I have since used these tools with nearly every client I work with, whether they have trauma histories or not. For assessment and treatment planning, particularly pacing, the Somatic & Energetic Resourcing tools are invaluable. Through the use of these tools clients can tell me where they're at, and how much they are ready for, without having to open up wounds.

It is always humbling for me to realize when I am out of touch with my own awareness. Usually this lack of awareness is most present when I am feeling the need to defend just how aware I truly am. This is amusing in retrospect, but somewhat painful when I realize this dynamic is occurring. Letting go of that darn ego's need to be right is trickier than I care to admit . . . and there's my ego again. . . . Therefore, I am so grateful for Debra's gift of this book. This is the sort of work that is studied, practiced, can fade, and can be revived over and over. It is easy to feel as if something is learned, and then move on to the next thing. However, what Debra offers us is a praxis; a way of being and a way of practicing which is very different than a technique.

As I followed along while Debra created this book, I experienced feeling a greater richness in the work I do with my clients. Even though I regularly use these techniques, watching this work develop refreshed my mind. Hearing how Debra explained the purpose and meaning behind each technique brought a new freshness to my use of the tools. Given her many years of therapeutic experience, she is able to offer great insights as to what to do when results of using these exercises come out in various ways with clients. She offers much wisdom as to what to expect, and what to do with the unexpected–as the unexpected does happen! When we stay in a place of openness and lack of judgment, listening and watching for what feels true and untrue within us and our clients, we can do our best work to guide those who come to us to find themselves. This is why we do this work, after all. I am so glad we have a teacher like Debra to keep us in our hearts as we guide others to be in theirs.

Tracy S. Reinhardt, Psy.D.
Licensed Clinical Psychologist
Practicing in Washington State

Preface

I knew back in 2009, when I revamped my original course, "Developing Resources from a Somatic/Experiential Perspective", this material was asking to be put into a book. Of course, the idea of writing a book was overwhelming at the time. I had meant to get back to writing it, but much happened in life that took me through more learning experiences, which ultimately have contributed to this book. If I had written it back then, there would have been very important information, about how to work with energetically aware and sensitive people, that would not have been included. I have to thank all of my colleagues who have suggested I write a book or asked if I had a book, for being the encouragement for finally getting this into print.

There have been many influences in my life that have contributed to this material. I have written one whole chapter where you can look over the major contributions to my journey. Here I would just like thank all of the programs, originators of those programs, clients, colleagues, and life events, both personally and professionally. All of you have contributed to my current awareness and capacities. Without all of you this book would not be what it is today. I especially would like to thank my courageous clients who have been willing to use these activities and step into reconnecting with who they are Authentically. Not always an easy task when the pain they had so creatively kept at bay, showed up, so they could clear it.

I have to warn you. I am always learning and expanding my awareness and capacities. So by the time you read this book I may have a new perspective on how to use these activities. This was one of the barriers to writing my first book. During my writing of this material, I have learned so much more that I feel I have to go back and do rewrites. There are a number of additions and rewrites I have already done, from information that showed up during the editing process.

I trust this book will find its way into the hands of people who can use the information at the time they find it. You may outgrow it or go beyond it at a later time. You may not find you can receive this information upon your initial reading. Later on what you read here may make sense. This work will plant a seed that will expand over time.

A number of clinicians who have taken my courses find they had more awareness of how this material works by using it over time, and by repeating the courses. I have found this work continues to teach me even though I have been practicing this way since 1991.

I am very grateful for the people who have contributed to the editing of this book. It has been a bit of a dance to balance writing in language that conveys Awareness, with academically correct writing. More on that in Chapter 1.

Thank you, Kathy Smith, for being on this journey with me. Your ability to edit this book with academic correctness in combination with conscious language has been invaluable. Thank you for learning these Somatic Resources many years ago, and for taking the conscious language course from me years ago. Who knew your learning these would have been so helpful all these years later. I still hear your voice in my

Preface

head, "If we change this to be academically correct will it still be energetically accurate?" And, thank you for making the time. We had some grueling editing sessions along with much laughter.

I would also like to thank Dr. May Johnstone, who offered her editing skills, and a different perspective. She is not a mental health professional but does energetic healing modalities. Thank you May, for hanging in there with me with the language that conveys energetic correctness. Your feedback helped me change some of the material so it could meet both criteria. Your suggestions helped this book read smoothly. I appreciate your time and dedication.

And, I would like to thank Dr. Tracy Reinhardt, another mental health professional. Tracy took my Somatic Resourcing course back in 2009, and is well-versed in academically correct editing. Without you, the information in the introduction about what to expect when reading text written in conscious language that conveys energetic correctness, would never have been written. I am sure many people who read this will be grateful to you for bringing to light the importance of that chapter.

Thank you Katy Murray, MSW for your last minute edits on such short notice in the EMDR Therapy sections. Your attention to detail is invaluable.

I would also like to thank my dear friend Mark Atteberry for taking my cover concept and turning it into a beautiful and captivating design. I have known him since high school and have watched his design capacities soar over the years. I asked him to design this cover because he has the unique ability to perceive what people are looking for in design. I have attempted to work with other designers before, and they often do not "get it". Mark and I collaborate well together. He also is a very talented musician. Thank you, Mark, for taking time out of your insanely busy schedule to contribute your talents.

Thank you Islam Farid for converting the e-version of the cover to print format. I appreciate your speed and technical skills.

Thank you to my publisher, Paul Burt, and Jennifer Geist, designer, of Transformation Media Books. You have been invaluable coaches and I have learned so much. I look forward to future projects together.

I would also like to thank all of you who are willing to learn these activities, and use them to return yourself to Living Authentically™, as well as facilitate your clients in Living Authentically™.

Table of Contents

Foreword xi
Preface xv
Introduction 1

Part 1

Chapter 1   How to Use This Book . . . 7
Chapter 2   My Awareness 13
Chapter 3   Stepping out of the Box and into the Art   21
Chapter 4   How Were Somatic & Energetic Resourcing™ Courses Created? . 35
Chapter 5   Assessment & Treatment Planning for EMDR Therapy & Other Trauma Treatments 47

Part 2

Chapter 6   Getting Started 61
Chapter 7   Self Awareness 75
Chapter 8   Reconnecting to Innate Signals Within   97
Chapter 9   Testing Safety & Relationship . . 103
Chapter 10   Containment 113
Chapter 11   Eyes Open/Eyes Closed . . 117
Chapter 12   Creating a "Felt Sense" of Resource . 123
Chapter 13   Recognizing Truth . . . 127
Chapter 14   Is This Even Mine? . . . 139

Chapter 15	Support in a Chair	145
Chapter 16	Developmental Foundation of Connection with Self & Centering	151
Chapter 17	Connection with Body, Self & Earth	157
Chapter 18	Connection Activities	167
Chapter 19	Centering	197
Chapter 20	In Conclusion	207

Resources & Recommended Readings . . 213
About the Author 215
Audio Publications 217

Introduction

Who Is This Book For?

This book will be useful for any mental health professional who prefers to work, or is interested in learning to work, experientially with their clients. Particularly for those of you who have found talk therapy to be less than productive in getting anything other than superficial change. If you are interested in developing your ability to perceive past what is said in session, you will find the more you use these activities, the more the activities will teach you.

These activities are also excellent for assessing a client's preparedness for trauma work. They will help you identify:

- Are they able to stay present?
- Can your client tell if and when they are dissociating?
- Will they tell you when they are dissociating, or becoming overwhelmed?
- Are they giving you clear and accurate information?
- Are they able to handle the strong emotions that may come up during the trauma work?
- What kind of internal developmental resources do they have?
- Is your relationship able to tolerate the trauma work?

I often share these tools with my consultees to identify who is appropriate for trauma work, and who is not yet ready. These same activities assist in preparing clients for doing trauma work. They can be used in conjunction with any modality for treating trauma, i.e.: EMDR Therapy, Lifespan Integration, psychodynamic therapies. You can use them to identify underlying life experiences and the core beliefs that motivate dysfunctional reactions. And, in some cases, just by using them your clients build a more stable foundation from which to address traumatic material, without being over-stimulated.

I originally developed this course for mental health professionals, and do recognize there are others outside the mental health arena who are interested as well. If you are reading this and are not a mental health professional, just be aware that these activities are designed to facilitate more Self awareness, more connection with Truth, and to support people in living more authentically from who they really are. There is a segment of the population who have created pretty elaborate and sophisticated systems to stay disconnected, to avoid feeling and overwhelm. These people may have severe trauma or neglect histories or some underlying neurological issues, and are often very intelligent and creative. If you run into this, then make sure to consult with a mental health professional to determine if they need to be referred to someone who specializes in treating trauma, *and* is trained to treat trauma through experiential activities.

Typically these activities are soothing and resource-building. But for some who have severe trauma and neglect they can be disruptive to the person's avoidance system. Not because they cause harm. But because they facilitate people getting reconnected to themSelves. The resulting symptoms just mean they have gotten in touch with things they have blocked or suppressed, and they require very subtle timing and pacing skills, and rebuilding resources in a delicate manner.

Introduction

These activities are just the beginning. There are three segments to my Somatic & Energetic Resourcing course. What I have shared in this book are the foundational tools. These are also tools that I can describe in a book format. Others really have to be done in person, or through experiential activities. There are many activities; this selection will get you started in building the foundation to do the more advanced work.

Part 1

Background and Preparation

Chapter 1
How to Use This Book

What You Need To Be Successful.

There are a few things to consider before reading this book that will help you to receive as much as you can from it. First, it is written as a practical, how-to manual. It is not about theory, research or trying to fit into the current mental health constructs. It is more about looking outside the box for new ways to use existing tools, and being willing to add some that are effective and often ignored. This work is intuitive and based on your intuitive capabilities. It is about bypassing linear constructs. It will support you in expanding your intuitive and awareness capacities. Because this work is intuitive in nature, there are no cookie-cutter answers, conclusions or results. And, what shows up is always useful information.

If you are looking for linear, predictable constructs you may find yourself frustrated in a number of areas. This work is about assisting clients to get out of limiting constructs, so building a construct to get out of a construct just creates another construct.

My next point relates to that last sentence. I have written this work in language that conveys awareness, not mental constructs. What is that? Language that conveys the accurate awareness of the information. Words and sentence structures are chosen based on the awareness they convey. This was a bit of a challenge when looking for editors. Luckily I have some good people who have that awareness capacity and are academically well-versed in editing.

When reading some parts, you may feel things don't flow. It may feel garbled. When this occurs there are some questions to ask yourself. First, are you using a definition of a word inaccurately? Is there a different definition of the word that will fit more accurately? Look up the word and see if there is a different definition that clears up the sentence.

If a different definition does not clear it up, the next question is, "What limitation do I have here that is preventing me from receiving this clearly?" Is there a mental construct you have that is blocking your ability to receive the information?

I will give you an example. I have been facilitating classes on a number of topics since the early 1980s. In 2011 I was facilitating a class for a program I was a contractor for. In one part of the class, I chose to read a short paragraph from the manual to convey the specific intention of the author. When I attempted to read the paragraph, it was totally garbled. My head spun and I could hardly speak. Something I had never encountered before. Luckily, I had been trained how to facilitate in class when this kind of garbled energy shows up. So I ran a clearing from the program and suddenly it was very easy to read. And, this time everyone in the room got it very clearly. The clearing I ran was about where the participants were unable or unwilling to be aware of and/or receive the information. Once the limitation was cleared, the information could flow easily.

There are places in this book where I know what I am writing just messed with a limiting construct in the mental health field, or is introducing a completely different way of operating. I know for many it will come across as not making sense. Which is actually a good sign. In those places, I will ask a question about how garbled that part was for you. So I am being very obvious. In other places a sentence may not seem to flow, so it may be highlighting a limitation. Let me give you an example. As Kathy Smith and I were editing, there would be places that would be very garbled. Once we cleared up how we conveyed the information, the material became very clear. We began to trust the garble and let it direct us to where the limitation was, and clear it up.

For some of you this may seem odd. Some of you will know exactly what I am saying. I had people both in the field of mental health and outside of it work on the editing, all academically well-versed in how to do sentence construction. All gave me feedback about where it did not flow, or did not fit academically correct grammatical structure. They gave me suggestions on how to correct it. In many cases the suggestions changed the energetic accuracy of the information. Yes, the suggested wording flowed better, but changed the intention of the awareness that was being conveyed. Sometimes I found a way to reconstruct the sentence or paragraph that met both criteria. Other times I could not, so I chose to stay with the version that conveyed True awareness.

Somatic & Energetic Resourcing

This work is designed to support people in getting free of mental constructs that are limiting them (definitions of self, roles a person plays, obligations people choose, judgments of self or others). So the work is both for you and for your clients. As you read, if you experience the information as garbled, not making sense; if you read the same sentence or paragraph over and over and don't get it; you may be applying an inaccurate definition of a word or words. Or, there is some sort of limitation in yourself interfering with your ability to be aware of the information. Once I recognized how limitations interfere with understanding written material it opened some amazing doors to information I previously could not receive. I use this awareness now with everything I read. I have had many clients and colleagues I shared this information with who have reported the same.

What a wonderful opportunity to clear up the definition or clear the limitation! The work is diagnostic. It will expose limitations. It also is an opportunity to clear those limitations. The activities help flush them out and build resources which will create change. So does the way the book is written! My other editor, Dr. May Johnstone, said she found it helpful to reread the material a number of times. She found that subsequent readings provided her with a deeper awareness of the material and how it works. Once I discovered how this works I have applied it to everything I read and have had some amazing doors open to information I previously could not receive.

Have you ever read a book written in language meant to convey True awareness before? There is a good chance you have not. So this could be a new experience for you, if you use it to your advantage. Use it to notice where you have limiting constructs and be curious about the blocks, what they are. If

How to Use This Book

you already have tools for clearing those blocks, use them. If you do not, get facilitation to do so. The more you clear out, the more effective you are in facilitating your clients.

If you really get stuck, I am available for individual sessions and case consultation. And I facilitate courses, both in this material and in developing Self awareness and clearing limitations. There are many tools I use to clear limitations that are outside of the current mental health constructs. They are often more effective and quicker. What I share in this book can fit inside the mental health construct but also pushes the envelope. If using the out-of-the-box tools helps you clear blocks so you can use the more in-the-box tools in your practice, I am excited to contribute.

I just thought I would give you a heads-up before you read this book. To let you know that where it does not seem to flow may be an indicator of something other than poor editing. It is a different way to read and a different way to write. Because of my conscious language training I can hear the limitations when people speak to me. It is really obvious to me. People are often amazed at how quickly I pick up what the issues are for them. It is just about learning how to do it. Pretty simple actually. Except for the learning-to-be-present all-of-the-time part.

So I invite you to step into your curiosity about what might be showing up to change, as you read. Have fun with it! It is always easier that way.

Chapter 2
My Awareness

After working in the field of mental health since 1977, here is my interesting perspective. When we are not living from who we really are, when we are choosing things in our lives that are not aligned with who we really are, symptoms arise. Our innate wisdom communicates with us through physical and/or emotional symptoms. These symptoms are a signal that we are choosing against ourselves; we are not living in alignment with who we are. We have gotten off the mark. When we cut ourselves our body knows how to heal it, and just does so. When we don't drink enough water we get thirsty, a symptom communicating. Eventually we get a headache, another louder symptom, because we did not listen the first time. If we continue to not listen, to not correct our choice, the symptoms get louder and we become increasingly disabled. We do things that are not True choice for us in order to fit in. We get anxiety and depression. There is a cascade of chemical reactions that takes place. We have changed our brain chemistry. If we don't get back in line with ourselves, the anxiety and depression get worse and can become intractable.

I have had the good fortune of choosing trainings and treatment modalities that have taught me to facilitate clients in experiencing their own innate wisdom. Here is a question I asked myself: How do I get out of thinking, and just be present and allow Truth to show up? Using many of those modalities over the years I have learned a great deal about how my thinking and my mental constructs, as traditionally taught in the field, completely obscured my ability to be aware of Truth and facilitate my clients back to their own innate wisdom.

I have been very alarmed to watch the field over the last 20 years dumb itself down with more intellectualization. Treatment modalities sanctioned by insurance companies have moved more and more toward cognitive, right/good thinking and behaving, instead of authentic Truth for each individual. It is more about mental programming of what is right and good instead of, Who are you? What is really True for you? What choices are you making? And, What is your innate Truth telling you about those choices? What happens when you choose *for you* instead of *against you*?

I was recently speaking with Dr. May Johnstone who lives in Scotland. She was asking about a biofeedback program as an alternative possibility to show clients the change they get from the energetic work she does with them. She said she had heard about a psychiatrist, Dr. Maarten Klatte, in the Netherlands who is doing more authentic work. He takes blood samples before doing any interventions. He uses the Sedona Method to create change, but any modality will work. Then he takes another blood sample, and both he and the client see how the blood cells have spread out from their previous clusters. He also reports significant improvement in blood pressure after using a clearing method. So we can actually see the body respond in a healthy way to people letting go of what is

My Awareness

limiting them. There is a link in the Reference material to his website if you are interested.

In *The Biology of Belief*, Bruce Lipton does an excellent job of showing exactly what occurs in our bodies based on how we choose to live; for ourselves, or against ourselves. He is a geneticist who used to teach the old genetic model that our genes predetermine what will occur physiologically. On sabbatical he had an epiphany that it is our environment, including our self perceptions and choices, that creates physical changes. When he returned from his sabbatical he applied for a job at Stanford University and presented his theory. They hired him, and he did research which validated his awareness. He clearly describes what occurs biologically when choosing for ourselves vs. against ourselves. This book is really easy to follow despite the detail he goes into. Lipton left Stanford because the information was not getting into the mainstream. He now writes and lectures independently. It is sad how structures refuse to adapt to new information, and how much money dictates what is sanctioned.

I have watched people get sicker and sicker with anxiety and depression in direct correlation to how they think. The right/good thinking, or trying to control their thinking and behavior, and making choices over and over again against what is True for them, leads to more intractable symptoms. They can clearly tell me the physical and emotional reactions they are getting from their thought or their choice, but they are so attached to the mental programming of how they should be, or what is successful, that they say over and over that they have no choice but to choose against themselves.

I have had the opportunity to work with a few people with potentially terminal illnesses. When I ask them what they are dying to get out of, they will give me a list of things that are not working in their lives. What is eye-opening is, when I ask what they are willing to change, some will say everything, and they start changing things. Some will say, "I can't change it", and will go on to give me a litany of reasons and justifications of why they "can't".

Those who have changed the circumstances that are working against them have tended to get better, and have often extended their lives and had a better quality of life than they had before. Some have died, but were happier, more at peace, until they did. Those who have not been willing to step out of their mental constructs and Self limitations, continuing to choose against themSelves, have continued suffering physically and mentally, living a poorer quality of life. They often live in fear for the rest of whatever is left of their lives.

We have all heard of people who have faced this choice point. Those who have gotten well have often said that it was a wake-up call. They really had to examine how they were living their lives. They made significant changes, and have become more and more joyful in living. They often say they were looking outside of themselves for their sense of well being, for what they should do or be, think or behave. They looked to family, friends, job, social, cultural and professional expectations, instead of becoming aware of Truth for themSelves from within. They became aware of how their choices were affecting their health. Most had some level of anxiety, depression and a sense of not being OK in their lives, even though they were very gifted and amazing people. They have often said their illness was the best thing that ever happened

My Awareness

to them because they realized they had not been living authentically, so they changed everything.

I recall that Tapas Flemming, who developed TAT®, received a diagnosis of cancer. She did one round of chemotherapy, and then asked her doctor to take 30 days to do some of her own work before the next round. The tumor was still there when she took the break. She used TAT® on everything she was having a reaction to. Her doctor giving her the diagnosis of cancer. Her reaction to the doctor's reaction to telling her. Her reaction to telling her partner and friends. Her reaction to their reaction to her telling them of her diagnosis. Her fear of the diagnosis. Her fear of the treatments. Everything. She went back to do the second round of chemotherapy, and when they checked the tumor, it was gone.

Why does this work for some and not for others? I don't often see people really doing clearing work about their reactions to everything that causes disturbance in their lives. And, I mean clearing work, not talking about it. They are different. Very different.

Dr. Bernie Siegel wrote about this in his book *Love, Medicine & Miracles* back in 1986. He began to notice a distinct difference in his patients based on the stories they had about their life, and how they responded to their surgery and overall treatment of their cancer. He sees his work as a surgeon as offering tools to buy people time to change their life. I highly recommend this book.

There have been amazing scientific breakthroughs showing us what the brain looks like when people have certain "disorders". Unfortunately there has been a jump to the conclusion that the changes in the brain, as shown by scans, is the cause of the "disorders". The brain scans are only showing the results of what occurs when people choose against themselves. There is a tendency to create treatments that manage the symptoms, shut the symptoms up, control and reduce the symptoms. It really has not been about restoring health.

I see it differently. When people are not living authentically, symptoms will show up physically and emotionally. There are many cases, baffling cases for many physicians, where people who became terminally ill, with no hope for recovery, got well. Each of those people changed things dramatically and began living in alignment with Self. In some cases these changes occurred quite quickly. In some cases it took time for the physical and emotional systems to repair themselves. I have watched many clients make this transition from looking outside themSelves for their well being, into allowing the Truth within to live them. (This is one of those places that is energetically correct and will probably mess with your mind.) Watching people step into living authentically is one of the most exciting and joyful aspects of my practice.

I attended an EMDRAC (Eye Movement Desensitization and Reprocessing Association of Canada) conference in Canada in the late 1990s, the exact date escapes me, where preliminary findings of treating Phantom Limb Pain with EMDR Therapy were presented in a Keynote address. They showed pre- and post-treatment MEG (magnetoencephalogram) scans from the University of Tübingen, Germany, clearly showing a significant difference in the imaging after EMDR Therapy which correlated to cessation of pain. A speciality protocol was developed and further research was done, including with war veterans. Patients had been previously treated with traditional medical care, including various medications, with no

My Awareness

results. Here is an example of change occurring from other than a physical intervention—addressing the emotions, sensations and negative cognitions underlying the pain and event(s) contributing to the pain. You can review the various articles, conference presentations and chapters in the Francine Shapiro Library listed in the Resources and Recommended Readings section.

So this course is about restoring clients to their authentic Selves. Facilitating them in discovering what is true for them. Holding the space for them to relearn to live for themselves instead of against themselves. It is not a mental construct program. It is experiential. So for many of you it will be a steep learning curve if you are not living aligned with your Self. Some of you may think you are living aligned with your own Truth, and may discover through these activities that you are not, or not entirely. When you are able to model living authentically, your clients will make much quicker progress. They will experience the "felt sense" of being with someone who is living authentically. This will be more powerful than any verbal intervention you can ever do.

Please note: I am using a small s as in self to delineate the personality or ego and a large S to indicate the being, soul, higher Self, or authentic Self.

We will be taking the *doing* out of the therapy. The activities are an exploration of where your clients are at in any given moment. *They are not a doing.* The activities are designed to create more awareness of what is really going on for your clients, not what they tell you. They are designed to restore their connection with innate wisdom. This kind of work is subtle, like Truth. Truth is like a whisper, like a gentle breeze and is often missed when the thinking mind is spinning fast and so noisily. It takes slowing down to notice the way the Self is communicating through emotions and body sensations. We would like our clients to pick up the initial subtle signals, and get back on track long before the two-by-four comes out and knocks them down.

There is an interesting paradox that occurs. The slower you go, the faster they progress. Of course this will not make sense to many of them, maybe not even to you. But this is how it works. You may feel pressure by the client or the insurance companies to hurry up, to get it done, because it costs too much. Does that make you feel expanded and free, or contracted and heavy? We will get to this tool in a bit. I have found that clients who are in a hurry often miss the subtle signals of Truth, so slowing down teaches them to notice how much they have been missing.

So I invite you to get out of your head and into your experience. To begin, if you haven't already, to practice from your *being* instead of your *doing*. To use the tools as a way for both you and your clients to discover who they are authentically, to strengthen their "felt sense" of being aware, their connection with their physical and emotional signals. To recognize Truth and to choose *for* themselves, instead of *against* themselves.

If we truly wish to reduce the suffering in the world, a return to living authentically will have to occur. How much more creativity would be available if people lived authentically? How much of this creativity would be available to change anything, personally, professionally, and globally? What if we as a profession stopped trying to fit into the insurance company box, and returned to helping people be who they Truly are?

Chapter 3
Stepping out of the Box and into the Art

This course steps out of the bounds of the traditional mental health practices. As many of us have known for many years, psychotherapy is an art. The profession has attempted to make it predictable and replicable. This has left many clients in the dust and feeling like they failed because they did not get results from the modalities used. Particularly from the cognitive behavioral models that are the current new fad in mental health practice.

The current trend is to go to evidenced-based treatment. Here is the problem with evidence-based treatment being the standard for care. When the research is done, the top 20% and the bottom 20% that do not fit the preferred results are thrown out. So the research will show what works for 60% of the population. Researchers call the 40% outliers. Then the modality is sanctioned, and now insurance companies are paying for modalities that are effective for only 60% of the population. When it comes to medications we are seeing new drugs come onto the market, and then within a few years many lawsuits are filed against the drug makers for the harm the drugs have caused. What if those who are harmed were the 40%?

Somatic & Energetic Resourcing

No one asks, What will work for the 40%? How are they different? What would work for them?

There are more energy modalities showing up that are having some good results. I am a bit concerned that many of the creators of these modalities are attempting to be sanctioned by the insurance companies so the treatment will be covered. Or those who are energetically gifted in working with clients are trying to get recognized by creating certifications, etc. so they can fit into the existing system. What is the downside of this? The insurance companies are about making money. They make decisions that often compromise very effective treatments.

For instance. EMDR Therapy is a very effective treatment, particularly for PTSD. For a client to get the greatest progress within each session, 75–90 minute sessions are recommended. Less than that does not allow the client to get through the desensitization phase. Shorter (50-minute) sessions have been found to be effective when using EMDR Therapy, but the full reprocessing will require more sessions (Marcus, et al, 1997, 2004). In many cases clinicians have to stop the client in the middle of very painful material and close the session down. The current reduction in time in the new CPT codes pretty much cuts the desensitization time down to 15 or 20 minutes. That often leaves clients in a really raw state. So take another 10 minutes off of that to try to stabilize them before they leave. That leaves maybe only 10 minutes of desensitization time, to be safe. They actually would get more done with the extra half an hour, could leave in a more calm state, and would not have to suffer another week with material that did not have a chance to clear in the session. It is actually retraumatizing to access that kind of painful material without desensitizing it before they leave a session.

So money is dictating poor quality of care. Yes, there are some clients who do not have significant trauma histories and can move more quickly through material. But for others, this kind time limitation can be brutal. The EMDR Institute and community moved from 50- to 80-minute sessions quite some time ago because we recognized how clients were being affected. We chose to learn from what we were seeing, and adjust to provide good clinical care. So, alternative modalities seeking recognition by the system can also be dictated to based on insurance companies making money, instead of good clinical care.

Here is the problem: over the last 38 years of practice, I have watched people trying to get recognized. I have also seen the profession become more and more rigid and controlled, particularly with insurance companies now dictating what they will cover and how much time we are allowed to see a client for. The bottom line for the insurance companies is to make a profit. It is not about assisting people in living authentically as who they are. There was a time, when I was a child, when insurance companies were not for profit. The goal was not to make money off the subscribers, but to pool resources so everyone had coverage as needed. The profession seems to have placed itself at the mercy of a money-making machine, instead of holding the integrity of using tools and systems that get real change for clients.

New innovators of change tend to work from awareness. They get an inspiration, begin to apply it themselves, share it with others. Then as they are getting more results, more is shared and more people are trained. For these new innovations to ever be validated and accepted and paid for by insurance companies can take as long as 20 years. By then whole new possibilities have shown up. People receiving only insurance-sanctioned treatment are not receiving up-to-date treatment modalities. They are only receiving what will make the insurance companies money. Many clinicians are getting training in 20-year-old tools, because that is how they can receive insurance payments. So the whole motivation is about making money, and not what is currently available that will return a client to their innate mental health.

There is no awareness of what is True (recognition of all the dynamics of what is going on), in insurance companies, licensing boards, and governing bodies. It is more about control and structure. Structures, rules, and boxes create limitation. There is not a capacity to perceive what is True in any given situation. No one is asking questions: What is this? Can we change this? Is there a different way to configure this that will help all parties involved? What does work for the client, for the clinician? What works for this client? What will help this clinician improve their capacities? Things have moved more and more to a right/wrong system; you fit or don't fit (and if you don't you are bad and wrong). Professionals have more fear that they will be judged wrong, instead of being helped in difficult situations. So creating a box for energetic practices will limit the possibilities in the long run.

Have you ever noticed it is the out-of-the-box people that create amazing changes? How those innovators go beyond convention, accepted thinking, because they perceive a different possibility that can't be seen from inside the box? Have you ever noticed how much they get judged by the people desperately trying to hold onto the box? Notice how they get attacked and often have to endure years, in some cases centuries, of judgment and criticism, until others are finally able to recognize the Truth? What if we got rid of the box and just did everything based on what is True in the moment, on true Awareness? Isn't this what the sages have been saying throughout the millennia? What if the mental health profession was about facilitating true Awareness?

Returning to Our Innate Wisdom as the Source of Choice

Are you really willing to step into change? I can't tell you how many clients I have seen who are so beaten down by the mental health profession by the time they get to me. They do not fit in the box and have adverse reactions to the standard treatments. They feel worse about themselves for failing in treatment. Once they learn how to recognize Truth for them, even if their Truth does not fit in the box of this reality, the whole world changes for them. They learn that trying to fit in the box, in the structures, and then judging themselves for not fitting, is why their symptoms are magnifying. They begin to realize their innate wisdom is communicating with them. The box is not true for them. And, the symptoms keep having to get louder and louder to get their attention. They have spent years, lots of money, and used many medications to try to shut up the symptoms, also known as their innate wisdom. As they learn how their own internal system communicates with them and begin choosing *for* themselves instead of *against* themselves, everything changes. They get better, they become healthier.

As I mentioned before, this is much the same as for people who have had life-threatening or even terminal cancer, who realize how they have been living against themselves. They change everything about how they were living, choose for themselves, and the cancer disappears miraculously. Their doctors cannot explain it. These people often say the illness was the best thing that happened to them, because it made them look at how they were living, and they began to choose differently. They stopped living from what others expect of them, from what the external world defines as success. They began living and choosing *for* themSelves, what works *for* them.

Mental health symptoms are much the same. Are people choosing *for* themSelves or *against* themSelves? Are they willing to look at what they have chosen and created in their life? Are they willing to change what is not working for them? Are they willing to make choices that bring joy into their lives? Are they willing to give up the structures, definitions, and reference points they have used to define themselves, that are killing them and creating their suffering? Are they willing to let go of these Self limitations and choose what is True for them? Even if it does not make sense, to them or anyone else? Do they know how to even perceive what is True for them?

Are *you* willing?

These are some of the things we will be looking at in this course. It may challenge everything you have ever done before. Yes, many of the tools you can use in the traditional box; but if you are really willing to assist your clients to get free, you are invited to step out of the traditional box and operate from Truth.

Restoring Innate Wisdom

This program is about developing awareness, the ability to recognize what is going on. To use questions to bring up more awareness, to use questions to take notice of which modalities could help clients change things. To be aware, instead of mentally calculate. If you don't know what that means when you just read it, you are in for a completely new experience. If you totally get it, you are way ahead of the curve.

This program is about restoring both your and your clients' ability to recognize your innate wisdom and choose from Truth instead of against it. There is an innate wisdom in each of us that moves us to health. Little kids have it (until the adults interfere and tell them not to listen to it). They just know and speak Truth all of the time. They are very generative and creative people. They are always busy creating, trying things out and applying what they experienced to future activities. They don't have a right or wrong about anything, they just get more awareness about what does or does not work and apply it to future activities.

Then, in step the big people. The big people tell them about right and wrong, to be right and good, and avoid wrong and bad. I have had many clients over the years who stay really stuck just because they are afraid their choice will be wrong. They have to know the end result before they will make a choice. They are unwilling to allow things to unfold, learn from what does not work, and apply it to the future. The amount of anxiety and depression I see in people just from clinging to the "be right/avoid the wrong" polarity, is absolutely insane. Where do we get this? From our parents, from our culture, from religions and spiritual traditions, from schools, from media, professions, from the social scene. I have watched people get sicker and sicker, including the mental health professionals, from being stuck in this polarity. I often wonder how much humanity would progress if we eliminated all of the right/wrong, good/bad boxes and used our innate guidance to direct us instead. Of course that would require us to be brought up and mentored by adults who supported us in staying connected with innate Truth.

The innate wisdom within each of us points us to the Truth of what works for each of us individually. What works for us may be very different from others. Our bodies heal themselves when we get a cut. We get physical and emotional symptoms telling us whether what we are choosing is True for us or not. But we have not typically received an upbringing where we are encouraged and supported to listen to our innate wisdom, and choose based on it. We live in a culture where we are encouraged to shut up our innate wisdom when it shows up as a symptom. We are told to use medication, instead of being curious about what those signals are telling us, so we can change what is creating them. Most people I have worked with over the years, both as clients and fellow professionals, don't have a clue how to read their own innate signals, let alone honor them.

So this course is about restoring our ability to be aware of what is True. It will start out with somatic awareness tools and move to developing an energetic capacity. Everyone's pace will be different in how quickly or slowly they progress through these. For those of you really attached to men-

Stepping out of the Box and into the Art

tal computation, you may find this quite challenging. It is much like having an over-developed muscle that is causing imbalance in the system because the opposing muscle has no tone. Do you know what the most prevalent addiction is on the planet? Ready for this? THINKING! So how much tone do you have in your Awareness muscle?

Are you willing to step into a totally different possibility? To open your Awareness? To step into the art of restoring innate wisdom?

Somatic & Energetic Resourcing

Remember:

> *"Minds are like parachutes.*
> *They only function when open."*
> *Sir James Dewar, Scientist (1877–1925)*

Activity for You

Please take a moment to write down what awareness shows up when I ask some questions. Notice I asked what *awareness* comes up. Awareness is different than thought or belief. I am not asking you what definition or mental construct you have. I am asking these questions for you to get in touch with the Truth within you. So please get out a piece of paper and something to write with, and write down what spontaneously shows up when you read each question.

- What does being a therapist, counselor, practitioner mean to you?
- When you are working with clients what targets are you aiming for, what are you looking to see change?
- How do you, as a practitioner, contribute to change?
- When you take continuing education courses, how do you choose?
- When you are working with people, are you focused on reducing symptoms, managing behavior?
- When you are working with people, do you see the innate mental health, the innate wisdom within them? Who they are authentically?
- Are you practicing authentically?
- Do you practice according to how external sources say you should? Or, to fit into the existing structure to get insurance money?

Is your practice set up to contribute to you and your clients, or to work against you?

Why am I asking you these questions before you continue on? This course is about living authentically. Through activities the course allows both you and your client to discover what it means to live authentically. When you are and when you are not. What happens in your clients' lives when they are not living authentically, and what occurs when they are? You as the practitioner can be a catalyst for change for them, or you can reinforce their Self limitations. When you are living and practicing authentically, your clients will receive benefits far beyond the techniques and activities you do with them in the office. They experience a "felt sense" resonance of what it is like to live authentically, just by being in the room with you. If you are living authentically.

Here is another way to put it. We have given our left brain all of the power. But our conscious mind can only process 7 bits of information per second, and it can only process things in a linear fashion. Our right-brain parallel processor can process a million bits of information per second. It can pull from anywhere at any time in any order. So by trying to change things based on left brain processing we essentially lock our clients into the same series of limitations. By doing any activity that gets out of the left brain and allows the client to receive new information, or information that is in the right brain, we can see quicker and more profound change. This is why things like EMDR Therapy, somatic activities, and energetic tools work so much better, even though some don't completely make sense. The only drawback is, a clinician or client can block their effectiveness by allowing the left brain to come in and not believe it will help, because it does not make sense. There is that pesky left brain again. This is why I invite my clients to do experiments. To suspend judgments and consider doing experiments, and see what shows up differently based on different choices.

Stepping out of the Box and into the Art

As you go through this material you will receive what you are capable of receiving at this time. This will be based on your life experience, your own Self limitations, and how much you approach the material as a set of mental constructs, exercises to do, or how much you approach it from an open space of receiving.

This is what I can tell you that will be an indicator of what you are able to receive at this time. If you have "aha" moments or feel more and more lightness or expansiveness, perhaps just some little tidbit to add to what you are already aware of, you are receiving. If you get irritable, judgmental, keep going to reference other things you already know, then you are running the material through your mental constructs and limitations. These constructs and limitations will reduce how much you can receive from what is available here.

You can use your judgments and irritation to your advantage. Anytime there is judgment, anger, irritation, then it is lie and/or limitation operating. Your awareness and ability to receive are greatly reduced. Anytime you read or hear anything that evokes these responses you have a wonderful opportunity to clear the limitation. Sometimes the sentences you are reading may seem garbled. If you clear the limitation that you are holding, you will find the same words make perfect sense. You may or may not find the information will work for you. It may or may not be new to you. But now you are in a neutral place of perceiving clearly what is there, instead of being reactive. Reactivity cuts off what you can receive. The really cool thing is, this is a shortcut for getting out of limitation. You might consider revisiting the questions listed above every 6 months or so and see what shows up.

Are you practicing authentically, from your authentic Self? What shows up? Are you practicing from mental construct and attempting to fit in the box? What shows up? What kind of clients show up in your practice when you are practicing authentically? What kind of clients show up when you are practicing from mental construct and trying to fit into external expectations? What kind of improvement do clients make when you are practicing from your own authenticity? And, when you are not?

I invite you to step into your authenticity and receive as much as you can. The more you play with these activities, the deeper your awareness will become of how these activities can contribute to change. When you find the material "isn't working," you are on the edge of a deeper awareness of how these tools will always show you what is going on in any given moment.

Enjoy the journey.

Chapter 4
How Were Somatic & Energetic Resourcing™ Courses Created?

This course has been through a number of evolutions. It was first presented in the late 1990's as "Developing Resources from a Somatic/Experiential Perspective". Later as I made changes and incorporated more awareness I called it "Somatic Resourcing 1, 2 & 3". I recently developed a 4-part series called "Living Authentically™" with a specific focus on assisting people to have the "felt sense" of their innate wisdom and truth. I included tools for clearing out what has been inauthentic, and then a section on creating from authenticity. I have consultees who began asking for the somatic information again to help them assess their clients' readiness for trauma treatment. As I began updating the information, I became more and more aware that the Somatic Resourcing course was also about living authentically. I began moving more toward teaching tools for getting the "felt sense" of aligning with innate wisdom.

As I have been revamping my Somatic Resourcing 1 course, one of my questions was how to solve the issue of practitioners not having their own resources. In my last update I designed the course to meet once a week and assigned the practitioners to do the homework for themselves, just like they would assign it to their clients. In this way they would become aware of what they had and what required rebuilding. Unfortunately many did not take advantage of the opportunity. They wanted the program to be another mental construct. When I was teaching the course in 2009 and 2010, I found some practitioners already had the resources to receive the material and employ it easily in their practices. Others did not have the connection to Self really required to facilitate others in the work.

So it looks like the Living Authentically™ Course may end up being a precursor to taking this Somatic & Energetic Resourcing 1™ practitioners course at some point. This way the practitioner will have developed the capacity to be aligned with their authentic Self. Living from authenticity is the foundation to being successful with this work. The real question is, how many practitioners are really willing to do so?

What Has Influenced This Course?

There have been a number of influences for the evolution of this program. About ten years into my career I was finding that very bright and motivated clients were not getting change with the talk therapy models I had learned over the years. They had a good grasp of the concepts, but they either could not get things to change or they forced themselves to act differently, which took a huge amount of energy, and they felt like frauds. The change did not occur organically and how they were acting did not feel true for them, authentically who they were.

So I began asking, "What will create the change they are looking for?" I learned much later in my career that my willing-

How Were These Courses Created?

ness to ask, "What else?", has been crucial to this evolving process. Through some friends I learned about The Hakomi Method developed by Ron Kurtz. At the same time a mentor of mine, who was trained by Carl Whitaker, called me up one day and told me about a very strange new program that was getting some remarkable results, called Eye Movement Desensitization Reprocessing, now known as EMDR Therapy.

So as is very typical of me, I started learning, about both. This was in 1991. I took the two-year program in The Hakomi Method. The strengths were their tools for developing Self awareness, timing, and pacing. And, how to read the structures in the body that indicated what had occurred during developmental phases. I learned how to access issues that were creating limitation, by learning to see how limitation shows up in the body. I found the developmental phases used in Hakomi rather broad, and focused on pathology, with very little attention to actual change. There were, however, very useful tools for Self awareness and accessing issues. I learned about bypassing the mental defense systems so clients could get to the Truth. This program was profoundly helpful in learning to work experientially and energetically, from a state of *being* rather than *doing*. Although I found The Hakomi Method had limits when it came to creating actual change for clients, it changed how I practiced. I learned to get out of my head and be in my capacity to perceive what is going on with a client. I could facilitate their awareness about what is True for them.

I am grateful I was already taking Hakomi classes when I learned EMDR Therapy. It made including the physical reactions, when targeting an issue, so much easier. I was acutely aware of what was showing up in the body and in the energy field as we were targeting issues during the assessment phase.

Somatic & Energetic Resourcing

I had so much more awareness of how still-unresolved material showed up during the body scan at the end in very subtle ways. This allowed my clients to clear out all of the disturbance.

Because of my experience in the Hakomi program, I was also acutely aware of how words and language were crucial to accurate identification of core Self limiting beliefs. It made accessing the negative cognitions easy. This is an area many therapists struggle with when learning EMDR Therapy, since our traditional training does not have the body-centered identification tools. Therapists often tend to discuss what sounds right from a mental perspective. When the correct Self limiting cognition is discovered, the client will have a visceral, physical and emotional reaction. Now you have all the components required to really get hold of the issue and change it.

In 2000 I attended a conference that included Gregg Braden and Bruce Lipton. Both were sharing information about how what we choose, what we think, what we do, affects our well-being. They introduced Robert Stevens, who had developed a language system for becoming more aware of the words we use and how they point to the underlying belief patterns that create limitation. I did a session with him and had a very interesting change. So, off I went to take his courses, and became a Language of Mastery Instructor.

This was profound work for increasing my sensitivity to the effect of words and what they create in a person's life. I had already become very sensitive to words from my previous training, but now limiting words just seemed to jump out at me and point me very quickly to where limitation was. I found that people did not get profound change from the tools

How Were These Courses Created?

offered in that program. They tended to try to pick the right/good word to try to change the issue. Of course this does not work. People were usually not willing to put the time into the processes the program offered to get to the underlying issue.

I did some of my own work with a Somatic Experiencing practitioner, giving me the experience of the pendulation system of that model. I found pendulation very useful to add to resource development for two reasons. It allowed clients to develop even more awareness of what is True for them by going back and forth between activities, perceiving how their somatic and energetic systems respond to each choice. And, it was also very helpful for really traumatized clients to learn they can regulate their own system and they can choose. Restoring their sense of having choice is a major milestone for change.

In 2005 I took the Foundation Training of the Bodynamic program which originates from Denmark. This program was excellent in identifying very precisely the various developmental phases, what each phase looks like in the healthy position (physically, emotionally and psychologically), what it looks like if there has been interference early in the phase, and what it looks like if there has been interference late in the phase. They have literally mapped all of the muscles in the body, at what age the muscle begins to develop tone, and what the psychological developments are at that age. The muscle tone, rigidity or lack of tone matched the emotional and psychological issues the client presented with. The focus was not so much on the pathology, as on how to build in the resource that was missing.

Somatic & Energetic Resourcing

This program is very detailed. So much so that people who have completed the whole five years of training are able to palpate all of the muscles in the body and have a complete picture of what the client's issues are, without ever doing a verbal intake. I had a mental health practitioner tell me that she had a client once who had a body map done, and when she got the records was shocked at how accurate it was. The body always tells us what limitations we have locked into it. Few mental health people know how to perceive this. It is not generally a part of our formal education, and certification bodies do not include it.

I discovered at the very beginning of the Foundation training of Bodynamics that the same activities used to build a resource could be used diagnostically. Putting people through the activity told me what resources they had and what they did not. So I use them diagnostically as well as to build resources. In this way the client learns experientially what they have, and what is missing. And, what they experience when they do not have the resource, and what they experience when they do.

This resource model was very helpful in assessing my EMDR Therapy clients' readiness for this kind of trauma work. In the early years of EMDR Therapy we found there were some people who were overwhelmed or destabilized by the desensitization phase of EMDR Therapy. A great deal of resource development work was built into the EMDR Therapy training. But most of it is from a mental position, from imagination, which I found to be minimally useful if they did not have these basic developmental resources. I began using somatic activities to identify resources a client had and assigning them to those clients who did not have them. This is the really cool thing about these tools. When you do them with clients, you know if they have the resource or not. If they do not, just doing them builds the resource. Then I began using the resource model of EMDR Therapy to strengthen the "felt sense" of the resource. I found people who were imagining they could do things, but did not have the "felt sense" of it. I often have worked with people who have had other therapists do the imaginal resource development and installed the imagination with bilateral stimulation. In many cases, they did not have the resource. Once we added the somatic activities, and they got the "felt sense" of the resource in their body and emotions, the bilateral stimulation really strengthened them. Bilateral stimulation is not required and there are other ways to strengthen the "felt sense" of the resource as well. Please note: Bilateral stimulation for some clients will be destabilizing. This is one of the things these activities will bring to light.

Over time I have used somatic activities from a variety of sources, as well as some I have created myself. I use them to assess where my clients are at, if they are even aware of what is True for them, how clear they are at communicating what is going on for them, if they are able to stay present or not, if they will tell me the truth, and if they are able to handle strong emotions that can arise when clearing traumatic events.

There has been some really good information coming out in the mental health field on brain research and what occurs when people, especially children, are exposed to trauma, including protracted periods of trauma. There have been some really good treatments for change that have shown up, like EMDR Therapy and Lifespan Integration™, and now more body-centered and energetic approaches are beginning to be recognized. There have been key elements in the field that actually work against changing things. Unfortunately, the insurance companies are trying to drive the field back to more mental computation, talk work that really is not effective in getting to deeply ingrained issues.

Here is the problem with the cognitive behavioral approach. If the client has developmental trauma, where the limbic system has been affected, or not allowed to develop correctly, the cognitive approaches do not work. You are attempting to use higher brain function to repair a lower brain issue. These limbic issues come from interference with innate developmental activities, neglect, abandonment and very early trauma. They can only be repaired with non-verbal interventions. It is very delicate and often slow work. Pacing and timing are crucial. People have to have the experience of recognizing Truth for them and having a "felt sense" of their own Self. This cannot be gained by talking about it. The brain begins to show changes when the experience is repaired.

Empowering Clients by Putting Tools in Their Hands

For me it is about: How do I empower my clients to create change for themselves? So I began asking more questions about what other tools were out there that allowed clients to clear even more limitation between the somatic and EMDR Therapy sessions we did together. That would also allow them to clear distressing material that would show up between sessions as part of the clearing process.

I researched numerous energy psychologies and chose to learn TAT® (Tapas Acupressure Technique). This modality

How Were These Courses Created?

has a number of steps in it designed to clear how people lock limitation into their system in a variety of ways. There are some similarities to EMDR Therapy, in that it includes ways to clear the body of what has been stuck and showing up as limitation and somatic symptoms. It uses a specific hold (a very light touch) that allows the energy to dissipate through the meridians in the body. The clients do the hold themselves. I taught it to my clients so they could use it on their own in between sessions. In general they got very good results. The down side was getting them to actually take the time in between sessions to clear things when something came up. A TAT® session can take quite a while to really clear through all the steps. Some people were not willing to make the time for themselves on their own.

This had also been the problem with teaching relaxation exercises and meditation techniques to clients. Some would really grab the activities and use them to get change, but most were "too busy" to take the time for themselves. I had designed the somatic activities I assigned to take short periods of time, so they could be used more readily during the day. This was much more effective. So I started asking what else was available that people could use during their day. TAT® required a hold that could not be used just anywhere. Some of the somatic activities could not be used anywhere as well. So what else is out there?

In my TAT® coaching group people started talking about Access Consciousness®. Eventually I got around to looking it up. It is obviously not a form of psychotherapy but many of the tools are very familiar, although put in a way that is more user-friendly for clients. I incorporated some of the tools and clients found them to be very helpful. And, they could be used on the spot, even during a conversation with someone. I don't often recommend their whole program to people, but there are some ways they frame things that are very helpful to some people. Particularly those who are energetically sensitive. I always take what works and leave the rest.

One of the most profound beginning tools was learning to notice the difference between what is yours and what you have taken on from others, that is not yours. My clients found these tools to be very effective and helpful in their daily lives. Especially those who are energetically sensitive. They have learned how energetically sensitive they are and how to use it to make their life work instead of being overwhelmed and confused. This is something that is rarely acknowledged or addressed in the psychotherapy field for clients and for clinicians.

The programs I have mentioned are the highlights, some of the influences. Many of them may have evolved since the time I studied them. There are many more than I can recall in this writing, and I am always learning more. I tend to take what works for an individual client and use it. I do not force myself into a specific construct. Every person is different in their timing and pace. My clients have also appreciated not being held to a particular box. I love seeing what people are doing to create change and share possibilities.

I have taken what I have learned from all of these modalities and methods, and from working with my clients over the years, to create this course series. It is a different way to work from the trend that Mental Health is taking in the US. Mental Health Professionals are being pressured to work from a cognitive, mental construct base. My point of view is that

How Were These Courses Created?

mental computation is what is *creating* the various illnesses. It seems that as we began to embrace more effective and being-state forms of treatment, the profession took a sharp turn back into mental computation. The art of psychotherapeutic change, the art of facilitating a client back to the innate wisdom within, is being stamped out. Insurance companies in the USA are limiting how much time a practitioner can spend with a client, so very effective tools for clearing limitation are being dropped, as clients do not have enough time in session to open the wound and allow it to fully discharge, and for their innate wisdom to do the repair work. They are interrupted in the midst of painful material coming up because they are out of time. The really sad part is, practitioners are buying into the limitation.

Luckily these somatic and energetic tools can be done in shorter sessions. They are designed to assess and strengthen resources. They can create some very interesting changes in a very short period of time. And, for those who don't get a change, you will have a very clear indication there is some really important foundation work to be done before addressing any traumatic material. The tools will also flush out those clients who are either not yet ready or not willing to change. Then the seed is planted for another time when they are ready.

I invite you to step into learning to be an invitation for change by *being* instead of *doing*. These same tools will be very beneficial for you as well, and can bring you more ease in session with clients.

Chapter 5
Assessment & Treatment Planning for EMDR Therapy & Other Trauma Treatments

One of the things that became clear to me when I took my first body-centered training, was how violent the intake process can be for a client. I know that sounds like a pretty strong statement. But many clients will agree, it feels violating for them. In traditional work, clinicians start taking a history and coming up with a diagnosis, within the first or second sessions. Very often because insurance companies require it. This occurs before the client and clinician have a formal relationship or have tested out their communication styles, and how they work together. Depending on the client's developmental history, attachment history, trauma history, this first step can be a rather violent interaction.

This is one of the many reasons I am not on any insurance panels. When I first meet a client, discovering how we will work together, and what they require to have a successful experience, is first on my list. What I have found is, these somatic activities give me far more information than I get by asking the client about their history. I can then fill in specifics about what occurred and at what ages later, to identify events for clearing that are still keeping them stuck. Honoring a client's timing and pace is a first priority to building a successful therapeutic relationship.

As I mentioned before, I was trained in Eye Movement Desensitization Reprocessing, now referred to most often as EMDR Therapy, in 1991, and became a Facilitator with the EMDR Institute in 1995. Dr. Francine Shapiro did a very smart thing at the beginning of the development of EMDR Therapy. She formed a network and asked those who attended the trainings to write up the results they were getting with the various populations and diagnoses they were working with. These results were published in the newsletter sent to all EMDR-trained clinicians. This was invaluable to the development of EMDR Therapy. Dr Shapiro strongly encouraged research early on and published her first study in the Journal of Traumatic Stress Studies in 1989 (Shapiro, F. (1989). Efficacy of the Eye Movement Desensitization procedure in the treatment of traumatic memories (Journal of Traumatic Stress Studies, 2, 199–223). For a comprehensive list of research for EMDR Therapy you can visit: http://www.emdr.com/general-information/research-overview.html. For information on current research projects visit the EMDR Research Foundation at: http://emdrresearchfoundation.org.

We began to see that some clients got significant change in short amounts of time. Almost miraculous. Others took longer. And, others would become unstable, emotionally overwhelmed, and in some cases dissociate. And for some, they did not appear to get change at all.

By the way, for those of you who don't know, EMDR Therapy its not waving your finger in front of someone's face to get them to move their eyes when they remember upsetting

Assessment & Treatment Planning

events. The bilateral stimulation part of EMDR Therapy is only used in some of the eight phases. Very often clients and untrained clinicians think the bilateral stimulation is EMDR Therapy. EMDR Therapy is an eight-phase therapy. There are some clients who may not move out of Phase Two, the Preparation Phase, for years, depending on their trauma, attachment and developmental history.

So, this brings me back to what we learned in the newsletter exchanges in the early days of EMDR Therapy. Of course, we began to look at the differences and develop more specific guidelines for selecting clients who are appropriate for the Desensitization and Reprocessing Phases, phases 4–6. We also began discovering and creating ways to develop internal resources that clients did not have. A whole Preparation Phase was created and expanded.

From April to June 2001 I attended the Foundation Training of the Bodynamic Program. I quickly became aware of the powerful change that could occur from embodying a developmental resource. I and my fellow participants had profound changes physically, emotionally, and psychologically, when experiencing the activities. I realized that these activities could also be used to assess what resources a client has just by having them do the activity. I began working with clients with a variety of experiential activities that create a "felt sense" of resource. I then added slow bilateral stimulation, taken from EMDR Therapy Safe Place Installation. The slow bilateral sets strengthen the experience without activating traumatic material. My clients had profound changes in a sense of internal stability, confidence and the ability to handle strong emotions.

Resource Development and Installation (RDI) was developed by Andrew Leeds and Deborah Korn (1998, 2002) to increase a client's ability to change their emotional and behavioral state by enhancing access to positive or functional memory networks. This ability to shift states was recognized as an essential skill for clients to experience the dual attention needed for effective reprocessing of memories in the phases 4-6 of EMDR Therapy. When this protocol came out I found it very cumbersome in comparison to my experiential format.

The RDI protocol asked clients to "think" about a time they felt a certain way, or think of people in their life, or think about images, symbols, etc., they experienced as a resource. Many of my clients did not have these reference points. Oftentimes they were in their imagination but the installation never translated to truly embodying the resource. I have had clients who did RDI with other EMDR Therapy clinicians who had installed imaginal grounding. When I had them do the somatic connection activities they had, for the first time the "felt sense" embodiment of what it is to be "grounded."

I am sharing this journey in EMDR Therapy because this is true for all forms of trauma treatment, really any treatment. It is imperative to identify what kind of internal resources a client has. What kind of developmental foundation they have. What kind of attachment history they have. Often when I speak with clinicians about assessing internal resources, they have no idea what I mean. How to assess resources, or how to help their clients develop them. This is much like building a house. If the foundation is not stable, the house will become unstable under stress.

Assessment & Treatment Planning

These somatic activities can help you assess what resources your clients have, if you use them that way. This means not just having your client do the activities, but noticing, can they do them with ease, is this capacity already intact, or do they need activities to build the resources with?

So what do I mean by internal resources? There are certain developmental activities and tasks that build a foundation for us to function in the world. When we have them, we have a sense of having a right to exist; we have the capacity to emotionally regulate; we have a sense of autonomy while still being in connection with others; we can assert our will; we can have our opinion and express it, even when others disagree, and change it when we get new information. We know what is True for us, even if it is difficult for others, respecting other people's differences at the same time.

There are very specific physical activities all kids go through, that activate muscles which are also involved in the emotional and psychological development of that phase. When that learning is interfered with early in the phase, you will see very little tone in the muscles and more passive or victim responses, or a diffuse sense of Self. When the learning is interfered with late in the phase, you will see more rigid muscle tone along with more rigid emotional and psychological responses, such as anger, aggression, rigid presentation of self. Sometimes you will see both, because there has been disruption or trauma throughout that developmental phase.

When we first added the Resource Development Installation to EMDR Therapy, we initially looked for instances when a client actually experienced the resource and strengthened it. In this case, they already had the "felt sense" experience of

Somatic & Energetic Resourcing

the resource. For those who could not come up with a personal experience, we had them imagine the resource. I have found this works to a degree, but most often, they do not have the "felt sense" of it. In this case, the resource can become more of a fantasy reality. You can often tell, because a client can experience the resource in your office but not on their own, or in a challenging situation in their daily life.

When you add in the experiential activity, and they have a "felt sense" of the resource, and you then install the resource (EMDR Therapy) or reinforce the activity (from other modalities), you will see it generalized to various areas of their lives. Often in some very surprising ways.

Assessment

What I found is that using Somatic and Energetic Resources was a more useful way to assess what resources your client has, and what is missing. If your client can do them with ease, they have the resource. If they struggle with them, get overwhelmed with them, get frustrated with them, they are missing the internal resource. I would rather know this in the beginning than find out when I am attempting to help them clear traumatic material.

For those of you who are EMDR Therapy trained, Somatic and Energetic Resources are used in Phase One and Phase Two. Doing the history-taking based on the Adaptive Information Processing model can be overwhelming for some clients. Why? Because when you do a history on life issues, and the individual events contributing to those patterns, you stimulate the issue and the client may have emotional and physical reactions. So you may need to move to the resourcing work before the Preparation Phase to create stability and self-regulation. I personally start with these activities before I do detailed history-taking because they are part of my assessment of how they will tolerate the history-taking process. That way clients have self-regulation and calming resources before we dredge up all those issues and memories.

If you are not EMDR Therapy trained I strongly suggest you start with the resourcing activities first, to assess your clients' affect tolerance for accessing distressing material. I suggest your initial intake includes basic information about symptoms, previous therapy and their success in it, current basic functioning, medications and a general history, without allowing them to go into details of the story. A checklist

Somatic & Energetic Resourcing

of potential issues can be useful, e.g., physical abuse, sexual abuse, growing up in an addictive home. This allows you to avoid details at this time, and gives you the big picture, while minimizing the activation. You will have enough information to make the diagnosis. If a checklist of symptoms for history taking brings up emotional overwhelm, you already know resourcing is required.

Once your initial intake is done, you can use the Somatic and Energetic Resources for further assessment and treatment planning. These activities will help you and your client to identify life issues that are causing distress, and flush out specific memories that you can target, when you are ready to do the clearing work. You can use whatever modality you choose to clear the targeted memories.

When you are preparing your client for clearing issues, and if you will be doing trauma work in particular, here are some things to keep in the back of your mind as you do the resourcing activities.

- Does your client have a sense of having a right to exist? What is their relationship with their Self?
- Do they give you clear and accurate feedback?
- Are they able to form a trusting relationship with you, with clear communication?
- Do they hide things from you?
- Do they try to please you?
- Are they honest, open-minded and willing to change?
- Do they have a support system and do they use it for support for themselves?
- What timing and pacing works for them? Not what they say works.

Assessment & Treatment Planning

- Are they able to tolerate strong emotions?
- Do they emotionally flood easily?
- Do they have self-regulation skills? Do they use them? When they use them, are they effective?
- Can they dual focus? Are they aware of what is going on for them, while engaged with others?
- Do they dissociate? Can they identify when they are dissociating, and communicate this with you?

Watch for how the activities prepare your client for the work.

Treatment Planning

The other very helpful thing about these activities is that they can help you build a treatment plan. Your initial treatment plan can be the assessment of internal and external resources. As you go through the activities with your client you can add to the treatment plan according to what shows up from the activities. I usually add Somatic & Energetic Resourcing to my treatment plan in general. It is up to you if you would like to list individual activities you will use to assess your clients' current resources. There is an example of my ***Practitioner Checklist*** at the beginning of Part 2 after Chapter 6.

You probably have other activities you already use with clients for building resources. The Somatic and Energetic Resources may sort out where your other skill sets will be useful. They may allow you to develop a "felt sense" of the resource from your other activities, bringing them from an imaginal place to a "felt sense" experience.

When you do these activities you will also find your client will spontaneously tell you about limiting beliefs they have about themselves, and events that are still causing distress. These are all targets to include in your treatment plan.

For those of you who are EMDR Therapy practitioners, when presenting complaints show up while doing the resourcing activities, you can start a EMDR Therapy Treatment Planning Worksheet on that issue, or just put them on a list to address, and do the worksheet later. If it is a specific event, then add it to an existing Treatment Planning Worksheet that you have already started, or put it on a general list and see what Treatment Planning Worksheet to add it to later on. This allows you to be consistent in clearing all the individual memories identified for each presenting complaint.

For those of you not EMDR Therapy-trained, use your current method for treatment planning to note these beliefs and events, to be cleared with whatever modality you use. I would recommend making a list of what shows up so you can recheck them later, after the clearing work, to make sure all of the issues are clear.

I have found these activities have flushed out memories and beliefs that a client would never remember in a verbal interview. Clients have often surprised themselves with memories and events showing up that they "thought" they had dealt with. They had managed and adapted around those memories and beliefs, but had never cleared them. So they never would have told me about them, because they "thought" they were over them.

Part of the learning curve for you is learning how to be aware of the unspoken. How to use the Somatic and Energetic activities to notice what is not obvious. What may be out of your client's awareness about their Self. How to be aware of the difference between conditioning they have bought into that is not true for them, (causing abandonment of Self in order fit in), and Truth. If this is new to you, I would suggest consultation or experiencing this work for yourself to accelerate your learning.

They Have the Resource but Cannot Access It

Your client may have internal resources they are unable to access because of traumatic material. You may see the resources show up rather quickly when doing the somatic resourcing activities.

Or, your client may be unaware of or deny having the resource. How often have you seen clients with really amazing capacities, but they are not aware of them or deny them, or refuse them? Sometimes doing resourcing activities will bring the resource into their awareness. Sometimes it will not. For EMDR Therapy practitioners, installing the resource may strengthen your client's awareness of it.

I have often worked with people who have many resources available to them, but they cannot see or receive what is already there. For instance: Clients abused as children who cannot identify anyone, ever, in their lives who appreciated them or liked them. They always saw everyone as hostile. Going through their lives year by year, we were able to find people who were attempting to connect with them, bring out their gifts. They just could not see it because of their defense structures. Once they realized someone was attempting to reach out, we could install that awareness and they could take in what was always there for them.

If installing the resource does not work, traumatic material may be blocking the client from taking in the resource. So, if doing the activities, and/or installing the resource, does not connect their awareness with their abilities, the resource may emerge on its own once the traumatic material is desensitized.

I have had many clients who had previous therapy and had done significant work building in skills. But, the client complained it was hard work to make themselves do the skills, or they did not feel authentic when doing them, or they could not get themselves to do them at all. I knew they had the resource, so we did the desensitization work. After the desensitization, they would come into session sharing numerous examples of how they were able to use the skills, organically, spontaneously, without thinking about doing them.

The important thing is, by using the Somatic and Energetic Resourcing activities you will notice the resources are in place, just not accessible. Just going through the activities will flush out what they have and what they do not. Doing the activities builds in what is missing and strengthens what is already there.

Part 2

Somatic & Energetic Activities

Chapter 6
Getting Started

A few things before we get started. These activities are to be used to discover where your client is currently operating from, what resources they have, and what is missing. They are about developing awareness; what your client is thinking, what they are choosing and what results they are getting from how they are currently functioning. It is an opportunity for both of you to learn what is going on for them. As I mentioned before, most often clients think they know what is True for them, but they are sharing that information based on the very limitations and deficits that are creating the symptoms. So when you do an intake they will only tell you what they think they know, not what is actually True for them. Why?

This goes back to what I mentioned earlier. Most will be functioning from left-brain limitation. Until we learn to ask open-ended questions to become aware of possibilities outside of our linear thinking, we will be stuck with seeing the same limitations. Clients will tell you what they think (linear left-brain), their limitations and stuck beliefs, patterns and viewpoints.

Somatic & Energetic Resourcing

This work is about facilitating clients in returning to their connection with their innate wisdom. It is not about reinforcing their ego, or personality, their left-brain limitations. If you use the activities for you and your clients to discover the difference between innate wisdom and ego/personality, you are using them correctly. If you use them to expand your client's connection to their innate wisdom, you are using them correctly. If you use them to facilitate your clients trusting their innate wisdom and allowing it to direct their lives, you are using them correctly.

The ego is very tricky and often uses activities that are designed to reconnect people with Truth, with their authenticity, to create more limitation and suffering. For instance, the emphasis becomes on doing the activities correctly and making them meaningful and significant, instead of fostering the ability to witness how Truth shows up and how limitation shows up. Once they learn the difference, they can then choose Truth instead of defaulting to limitation.

Our clients are often very bright and creative people who have used their talents and capacities to adapt around limitations. So they have built a cognitive system to adapt, and those very adaptations are not Truth. The adaptations begin to crumble because our innate wisdom will always prompt us to Truth. So people become symptomatic as the innate wisdom within tells them that the constructs they built to survive are no longer useful. It is time to let go of them and return to innate Truth. Unfortunately they make up a story that there is something wrong, and go to a professional who validates that. The only thing wrong is, they are not living aligned with what is True for them. The symptoms are prompting them to be who they truly are.

Getting Started

So when they come for treatment, they tell you the constructs they are living by that are not True for them. They are not aware of what is True for them. They do not know how to be aware of what is outside their linear left-brain limitations. So I would suggest you do not take what they tell you at face value. This includes people who have been doing self-awareness programs. There is a difference between *doing* self-awareness and *being* Self aware. The activities in this program are designed to assist both of you in seeing what is actually going on for them, how their innate wisdom communicates with them, and to allow new possibilities the right brain is aware of to show up. It is a joint venture in assessing and inviting Truth.

Begin by introducing the **Self Awareness** activities as a way for both of you to see what is going on below the surface; there is no right or wrong, good or bad, correct or incorrect. The activities will just point to the truth of what is there and what is not there. This is the initial assessment part of the activities. Can the client name a sensation, or not? Can they name an emotion, or not? Do they have a "felt sense" connection with their body, or not? Are they aware of their physical and emotional signals when they are talking to you, or not? Do they stay connected with themselves when they are interacting with you or the world, or not? Are they able to contain strong emotions, or not?

Over time you will develop the ability to witness what is going on. The more you work with the material, the more awareness you will develop. The less you do with it, or the more sporadic you are with it, the less your awareness muscle will develop.

Initially these activities are useful for assessment, and then they can be used to build resources. If clients don't have the resource, using the activity, according to each activity's prescription, will develop the resource. If they do have the resource then just move to the next activity to assess if they have that one.

If You Don't Have It They Can't Get It

Here is something to be really aware of; if you do not have these capacities and resources yourself, then you will tend to read the scripts in a stilted, "from your head" manner. This will not really facilitate your client in the activities. And, you will have difficulty assisting them in developing their awareness and resources. This is why I set this course up so you are also practicing for yourself each week. You will learn what you have and what is missing. You will have an inside awareness of how things develop and change. This inside awareness will be far more instructive than any attempt at doing these activities from thinking or doing them "right". You will develop a more somatic and energetic capacity to discover what is going on with your clients.

Here is another really important piece. If you don't have the resource, then your client does not have the model to entrain from. We become the anchor, the model. They get a "felt sense" of what it is like to be with someone who does have awareness, the internal "felt sense" resources. It allows them to compare and contrast the difference in the various people in their lives. If you are disconnected then you will only convey a mental construct, not an integrated model of what it is to be operating from innate wisdom.

So please do these activities yourself until you experience the "felt sense" of your own inner wisdom. It is OK to be on the learning curve with your client. We all have had to do this when learning new things. And, this kind of work is very subtle and very powerful.

But I Don't Wanna

If you find yourself wanting to give up, not having the time, allowing everything else to be more important than being connected with your Self, congratulations! You will have an inside view of what it takes to *truly face* where you have been disconnected and how powerful your autopilot is. Be gentle with yourself and your clients. Be encouraging. If you drop off, just pick it up again. If your clients drop off, take a little time at the beginning of each session to do the activities. This will get them connected with their innate wisdom, then you can see what shows up. I have one colleague who is glad to guide her clients in session because it means she too is practicing and strengthening her own resources.

When your client does not want to do the activities on their own, you can just do them in the office. Just make sure to let them know this will prolong the time it takes for things to change, for them to have mastery over their life.

I explain to my clients that the neural pathways they have developed have been about disconnection. The pathways are much like a very deeply rutted road. It takes time to build new ones, pathways of being connected to Self, and for the old ones to atrophy. Just imagine driving down a deeply rutted road. You can pretty much take your hands off the wheel and the car will just follow the ruts. If you suddenly decide this pathway is not getting you to where you would like to go, you will have to really crank hard on the wheel to get yourself out of the rut and cut a new pathway. The next time you go down that same pathway you will again have to crank really hard on the wheel to get out of the rut. It will take time, choosing to divert yourself to a new pathway again and again, for the new pathway to become easy to access. And as you use the new one more often, the old one begins to fill in, grows over and becomes less active.

Here is another example I use. Let's say I go into your kitchen and rearrange your cupboards. A while later you go into your kitchen for a glass of water. Where do you go? The old cupboard, of course. Then you search for which cupboard the glasses are now located in. The next time you go into your kitchen for another glass of water, where do you go? The old cupboard, of course. There is that autopilot, that well-rutted neural pathway. So you open the cupboard, have a moment of irritation, exasperation, recognition (depending on your disposition), you close the cupboard and go to the new location. Then you go into the kitchen another time for a glass and you get to the cupboard, grab the handle, start to open it, but remember this is the old location. So you let go of the handle and go to the new location. The new pathway is beginning to form. The next time you go to the cupboard, you begin to reach for the handle and suddenly recall the new location. The new pathway is getting stronger. The next time, you start heading in the direction of the old location, but recall as you are heading that way and divert yourself to the new location before you get to the old. The pathway is getting stronger. The next time you go in, you go to the new location. The pathway is now developed.

Getting Started

My clients find these examples helpful in reducing their expectation for things to happen immediately. There are times these activities create really rapid, spontaneous change. There are times it takes some consistent repetition for people to get out of unconsciousness, out of autopilot. Those who are really invested in not being aware, in intentionally cutting off their awareness, may have the steeper learning curve. This can also point to secondary gains for staying unaware that have to be addressed.

Compare and Contrast

Set these activities up as experiments, as a way to see the difference between when you are connected and when you are not. By comparing connection with disconnection, authenticity with externally driven choice, and physical and emotional signals that show up when clients choose for themSelves or against themSelves, your clients will have a much clearer awareness of what is True for them. They get more clarity about what signals show up, depending on the choice they make. This is far more powerful than talking to them about it. As I mentioned before, people will talk a good line, but when we actually compare and contrast, the Truth shows up, and they are often stunned by what they discover. This "felt sense" awareness is more powerful and motivating than any mental construct.

Slippery Slope: Awareness vs. Doing

There is a slippery slope to any tool. Often people make the tool meaningful and significant. Like it will be the thing that will fix them. Watch out for this. These are just tools that help reveal what is going on, and they happen to create change because of the awareness, the new choices. Are they *doing* the activity or *using* it to perceive where they are at when they use it?

I said to a male client of mine once: These are just tools, like screwdrivers or hammers in your tool chest. They are used to facilitate something, change something. If you use the hammer to hammer in a nail, do you make the hammer meaningful and significant? Will it be the savior of your project? Do you always expect the same result from it? Does it always drive the nail in perfectly? And, if it does not, do you throw away your hammer and say it did not work? Or, do you sometimes hit the nail a bit off and have to make a correction?

Often I hear, "It didn't work." I ask, "What do you mean by, it didn't work?" They often say, "I really felt connected in your office but I could not feel it when I did it at home." To which I reply, "It sounds like it worked perfectly!" They always get a puzzled look on their face when I say this. "It sounds like you learned that you were very disconnected at the time, and there was something going on that you were not yet aware of, that was causing the disconnection. Give yourself a chance to learn from the activity instead of going into conclusion about what should have shown up, or using it to make yourself wrong."

Did You Get the Clue in That Last Paragraph?

When we take the "looking for results" out of the activities, they work really well. When people are attached to outcomes and what the right/good response is to the activity, or how it was before (referencing the past), the activities appear not to

Getting Started

work. But they actually are working. Are you aware of what creates suffering from what I just wrote in this paragraph?

Does your thinking feel a bit scrambled? Are you having difficulty figuring this out? There you go thinking again! That pesky left brain. This is where the learning curve is. How to spot the underlying limitations from the activities. Not to figure them out. Not to look for a predictable result. To instead choose a tool for changing the limitation. To ask open-ended questions like, "If you already had this resource what else would you be aware of?" "If you already had this resource, what would you be aware of that your limited left brain cannot recognize?" Again, not to get an answer, which would engage the limited left brain, but to invite your innate wisdom to bring awareness in its own timing. Yes, learning how your innate wisdom communicates with you, so you can work from awareness, trust your awareness, and facilitate your clients to live from awareness, can be a steep learning curve.

I realize those last two paragraphs may feel really convoluted. Bear with me. This is about awareness, not about thinking. It is a different way to work. We are taught to figure things out, to make sense of things. Again, our left brain can only process 7 bits of information per second. By using these open-ended questions, asking your innate wisdom, and learning to allow awareness to show up in its own timing, we bypass the linear limitation and open up to some pretty miraculous results.

Activities, Tools & Scripts

In each of the following sections there is an initial explanation of an activity and what it is designed to help with. There is also a description of how to do the activity, what the activity could reveal, and in some cases a script. I have included examples of homework forms I give my clients to fill out and bring back to session. This is mostly just an anchor for them to take action, but for some clients it is a very useful tool for discovering more and more about themselves.

I am including an example of my **Practitioner's Checklist** you can use to help you keep track of the order to do the activities in, when you assigned them and when your client reported doing them. The order is designed to progressively assess what is going on, develop clear communication and relationship, learn about your clients' resources and create a progressively more coherent sense of Self and authenticity.

I also include scripts for some activities The scripts are written in neutral language, and changing the language can change the results. Watch to see if clients have difficulty with the language. This could be diagnostic in itself. Very often clients who have created very intricate protection devices, or have a sense of never really being seen, or never having an authentic connection with others, will get very "in their head" and want to argue semantics. This is diagnostic.

Please do not change the language. If you start adding descriptive things or images, you may be inserting your own stuff and you will not get a clear read of what your client is experiencing in the moment. I have gotten pretty concrete in the writing of the scripts, including the amount of time people should pause. I was finding that some therapists were just reading the script, disconnected themselves, without allowing time for the client to notice their own experience. If you already have the capacity to allow the space and time for people to witness Self, go with what you are aware of.

If you are interested in using the forms I have created for this course, you will find details at the end of the book on how to purchase them.

How Do I Know Which Ones to Use?

The activities are designed to build on one another. They are in a progressive developmental order. For instance, if you or your clients are not Self aware 24/7, then you will have limited improvements, and in some cases no improvements, from subsequent activities. Using them in the order presented in this book will offer the best and most consistent results. The ***Practitioner's Checklist*** also lists the activities in developmental order. I suggest you only introduce and assign your client one activity per week. Assigning more than one can overwhelm and confuse clients, and decreases the possibility of them following through. If you do the activity in session with a client and they clearly have the resource already intact, then go to the next one.

Time to start.

Somatic & Energetic Resourcing

Debra A. Littrell
Transformative Spirit, LLC

Somatic & Energetic Resourcing I™
Practitioner's Checklist

Simple Activities   Client's Name: _____

Self Awareness - Simple	Date Assigned:	Date Completed:

Reconnecting w/ Innate Signals	Date Assigned:	Date Completed:

Testing Safety & Relationship	Date Assigned:	Date Completed:

If your client has difficulty with emotional overwhelm, add Containment.

Containment	Date Assigned:	Date Completed:

Eyes Open/Eyes Closed	Date Assigned:	Date Completed:

Recognizing Truth	Date Assigned:	Date Completed:

Is This Even Mine?	Date Assigned:	Date Completed:

Support in a Chair	Date Assigned:	Date Completed:

Sitting Connection - Simple	Date Assigned:	Date Completed:

If your client has difficulty with Sitting Connection, go to Sit Bone Connection and then Sitting Connection.

Standing Connection - Simple	Date Assigned:	Date Completed:

Centering - Simple	Date Assigned:	Date Completed:

Once your client is able to be proficient at Simple Self-Awareness and Connection Activities, have them switch to Integrative Self-Awareness and Connection Activities. These activities have more detail in how the physical, emotional and cognitive parts of ourselves affect each other.

© Copyright 2013 Debra Littrell All Rights Reserved. You may make copies to use in your own practice with your clients only. Otherwise this material cannot be altered, copied, or translated without the express, written permission of Debra A. Littrell.

Figure 1.1: Practitioner's Checklist
Page 1 of 2

Getting Started

Somatic & Energetic Resourcing I™
Practitioner's Checklist (cont.)

Integrative Activities

| Self Awareness - Integrative | Date Assigned: | Date Completed: |

| Sitting Connection - Integrative | Date Assigned: | Date Completed: |

| Standing Connection - Integrative | Date Assigned: | Date Completed: |

| Centering - On the Floor | Date Assigned: | Date Completed: |

| Centering - On the Ball | Date Assigned: | Date Completed: |

© Copyright 2013 Debra Littrell All Rights Reserved. You may make copies to use in your own practice with your clients only. Otherwise this material cannot be altered, copied, or translated without the express, written permission of Debra A. Littrell.

Figure 1.2: Practioner's Checklist (cont)
Page 2 of 2

Chapter 7
Self Awareness

Self awareness is the key to self empowerment. Self awareness enables us to choose our actions, instead of reacting from automatic unconscious programming. Let me be even more direct here. This is the difference: It is about being aware of how Innate Wisdom communicates with us and directs our lives. It is not about the ego or personality. People's egos, or personalities, talk them out of being in Truth. Self awareness is about facilitating your client in becoming aware of their innate Truth. Self awareness provides many benefits for both of you in session, and especially in preparing to do any sort of work to clear traumatic material.

In my previous version of this program I called this Mindfulness, modeled after what I learned in the Hakomi Method training. We used mindfulness to learn how our somatic and emotional signals communicate with us. Communicate what is right for us. Let us know what is going on with other people. Now that mindfulness has become fashionable, I have had both clients and consultees talk about mindfulness as a disconnected mental activity. They do the activity, may have been doing so for some time, but have absolutely no Self awareness. No awareness of what their physical and emotional signals are communicating to them. No awareness of their own innate language. So I have renamed this section to reflect the actual intention of the activity.

Essentially, mindfulness has become an ego-directed activity. Instead of an activity facilitating a person's return to their innate wisdom. As often happens, the ego will take information and tools to facilitate reconnection with Truth, and twist them into a *doing* activity that perpetuates the ego. It is a slippery slope. And, this material is in danger of being used in the same way. So please be aware that when using these activities, it is about reconnecting with innate wisdom.

By using these activities at the beginning of treatment, a number of very useful things occur. First of all, you and your client start right from the beginning working as a team. If you approach these activities with your client from the perspective of you not knowing anything about them, and what is True for them, and wondering how much they are already connected to their own Self awareness, you are already creating a collaborative relationship with them from the very beginning. Having a resourceful relationship with your client is imperative before treading into trauma work. This kind of collaborative work gives them an opportunity to learn about you, and to learn how giving you accurate information will help both of you tread through murky and often painful work when addressing trauma.

You and your client begin to learn what physical and emotional signals show up when they are aligned with who they are, and when they are not. You both learn what skills they already have, and what has to be developed. It sets the groundwork for them being able to give you clear information, both

Self Awareness

during trauma work and also between sessions. Self awareness will give you an initial clue about where your client is operating from developmentally. Have they developed an ability to witness Self? Do they know what is True for them? Do they choose based on what is True for them, or from external expectations or obligations that may be detrimental to them? Are they able to stay fully present, even when strong emotions show up? Are they able to tell you when they are losing their connection to Self?

Comparing and Contrasting

Warning. This section may not be left brain compatible.

First, it is important to become aware of whether you are being aware or not being aware. Then, becoming more aware of the kind of choices you make when you are aware, and when you are not. You can compare what physical and emotional signals show up when you are aware, and when you are not. (If you are having difficulty perceiving this, there is stuff to clear. Once you clear it, this will make perfect sense.)

Comparing and contrasting between awareness and unconsciousness brings in many possibilities. For some clients, they immediately use it to their advantage and use the activities to increase the amount of time they live in awareness. For other clients, it will flush out how much they are not aware and when they are not willing to be aware. This is very important diagnostically. It can point you to where to go next. The work with your client may be in clearing the payoffs for being unaware. For not choosing to choose.

I often tell clients, not choosing to be aware, not choosing to choose, is still a choice. One way or another you are choosing. The question is, "Are you willing to step out of no-choice and into changing things? And if you are not, what if you just owned you are choosing not to choose, until you choose differently? Isn't that a more empowering place to be?"

These questions allow you to explore with your client how choosing and not choosing create what shows up in their life. They can explore where they choose to choose, and how things show up when they choose. And, to explore where they choose not to choose, and how things show up when they choose not to choose. Did you get that? If it was murky there may be something to clear. This is about comparing and contrasting to bring more awareness. To practice being in a witness state instead of caught up in the content.

The majority of my clients really use this to their advantage. I am not asking them to choose differently, just to notice what occurs based on what they choose. Most people find that once they become aware that they have not been operating from awareness, and not choosing *for* themselves, they begin to change. Some clients will initially say they will choose not to change, and then come back next session and have changed things. Why? I did not challenge them about it, or blame or judge them for it. I merely suggested they notice what occurs and play with the difference.

Some have not chosen change. Some have stopped treatment when they are faced with the awareness, that awareness is a first step to change. But I have encouraged them to just own that is what they are choosing, so they also know they can change it at any time. Maybe in a few weeks, maybe in months, maybe in years.

This is not about judgment, it is not about resistance, it is not about expectation. If you do it from a place of just collaboratively exploring and being in allowance, much can change when they are ready.

Use What Does Not Appear to Work to Your Client's Advantage

I have had clients get very defensive. Great! This has been a wonderful opportunity to ask, "What did you just hear me say?" They usually tell me something completely different from what I said. They filtered it through their own Self limitations. So I assure them that is not what I said, and ask them what physical and emotional signals they got from the thought they just had about what I said. (More on how to work with this later.) Then I go back and say what I said again. They often are able to hear it more clearly. Then we get to do more exploring of how what they hear goes through their belief system and what shows up.

The more you use awareness tools in the office, the more change can happen spontaneously both in session and outside. It can be very motivating for clients to do the activities outside of session, to assist them in expanding their frequency of self awareness, and to use the tools when they notice they are disconnected.

Self Awareness—Simple

Start with *Self Awareness—Simple*. The simple script asks your client to report sensations they are experiencing in their body, emotions they are experiencing, and the *qualities* of their thinking. The first time you do *Self Awareness—Simple* with your client, stop after you guide them through the section on body sensations, and ask them to tell you what they are experiencing (eyes remaining closed). If they are able to name sensations, they have a well-developed body ego, and their early developmental years may have been healthy. If they are unable to name sensations their body ego is not developed. Their early developmental years have been compromised. They may have had developmental trauma, physical neglect, emotional neglect; they may have grown up in an addictive home; they may have experienced shock trauma.

Then move on to emotions and again have them tell you what emotions they are experiencing. Again, if they are unable to name emotions, they have had early developmental interference. Sensations and emotions are the base of our experience in early childhood, before the higher centers of our brains are developed. All experiences are remembered physically/emotionally. Children who are left alone for prolonged periods of time will not have the basic ability to read their physical and emotional signals, such as hunger, tiredness, knowing what is right for them.

Then move on to quality of thoughts. People often get caught up in *content* of thought and are other than aware of the *quality* of thoughts and what these qualities are telling them. What is the quality of their thought? Are their thoughts fast or slow, evenly paced, or darting around, or are they still? Are they

Self Awareness

more about the past and future, or are they right here in present time?

Developmental Impairments—Can't Name Sensations & Emotions

Clients who have difficulty with naming sensations, emotions and thought quality will require your help. Repeating this exercise in the office at the beginning of each session is important. Slow them down and encourage them to wait for the word that best describes their experience to come up on its own. Avoid giving them the answer. If you are going to assist them, give them general examples that include a range, for instance (physical) is it tight, loose; warm, cold; or (emotional) sad, happy; mad, calm. Use basic examples. The more they can name a sensation and emotion the more they will be able to integrate what they are learning (Vygotsky). You will be assisting them in developing body ego.

For clients who are having difficulty with naming sensations and emotions, add the prescription for them to write down the sensations and emotions they experience. Educate them about brain plasticity and how challenges keep our brain healthy and create success in our lives.

You will often get resistance because this is such a challenge for them. The challenge is the rebuilding of neural pathways, new circuitry. Most people are unaware of this, and if they have not had the fundamental developmental physical activities of creeping, crawling, cross-patterning that build these neural pathways, they will try to move away from challenges. Encourage them to see the challenge as a good indication they are making progress. The challenge they are experiencing is the forming of new neural pathways. I often find my clients become more motivated when I explain to them that they are just building a new road to run on that will give them more awareness.

Developmental repair work is slow, and often clients expect quick fixes because of media programming they have experienced. It is often tedious work and it *does* pay off. Contracting with them to practice consistently for 3 months is helpful. If they require shorter contract times, start with one month and help them identify what is different at the end of each contract period, then set new targets. Explain to clients that the frustration they are experiencing is an indication they are building new neural pathways. This is a normal part of learning, of developing the circuitry in their brain that was either compromised or never developed.

Please DO NOT make the sensations, feelings and thought qualities meaningful and significant. This is not about creating a new limited box for them to live in. It is about expanding their awareness. Every time we put definition to something, we create limitation. People put it in a box and then reference that over and over as what is true. This is just another limitation.

Self Awareness & Self Discovery

These activities are about Self discovery, Self awareness. They are about your clients learning how they communicate with themselves, mind, body and spirit. Each person will be different about how the communication shows up, and how it shows up over time, as they let go of more and more limitation. What a sensation is signaling in this moment, and where it is located, will be different another time. It is about allowing them to connect with their authentic Self, so they are always in the flow of what is True in every moment.

Somatic & Energetic Resourcing

Self Awareness Exercise—Simple (Script)

I invite you to close your eyes.

Scan your body.

Notice what physical sensations are present.

Notice what areas are comfortable and,

What areas are other than comfortable.

> *(Give them 2–3 seconds to notice.)*

Turn your awareness to the areas that are other than comfortable.

Notice what sensations tell you this is other than comfort.

Too hot, Too cold,

Is there too much pressure or tightness,

Or is there pain?

And if there is pain, notice the quality of the pain.

Sharp, Dull, Constant, Or does it come and go.

> *(Give them 2–3 seconds to notice.)*

Knowing you don't have to do anything about this, just notice what's there.

> *(Give them 2–3 seconds to notice.)*

And now turning your awareness to areas that are comfortable or at least neutral,

Notice what sensations tell you this is comfort or neutrality.

Self Awareness

Noticing the temperature,

How light or dense each area might be,

How loose or firm your muscles are,

How relaxed each area is.

> *(Give them 2–3 seconds to notice.)*

Just taking a moment, enjoy your more comfortable sensations.

> *(Give them 2–3 seconds to notice.)*

And now I invite you to turn your awareness to your emotions.

Noticing what emotions are present.

Noticing if you are experiencing more than one emotion.

And if you experience more than one emotion,

Notice if they are similar or congruent,

Or if they are opposites or other than congruent.

> *(Give them 2–3 seconds to notice.)*

Again knowing you don't have to do anything about them,

Just notice what you are experiencing.

> *(Give them 2–3 seconds to notice.)*

And now turning your awareness to your thinking.

You can notice what you are thinking.

Somatic & Energetic Resourcing

And more importantly notice the quality of your thoughts.
Are they fast or slow or evenly paced,
Do they dart around,
or are they still.
    (Give them 2–3 seconds to notice.)

And noticing if they are about your past or future,
Or are your thoughts right here in present time.

(Give them 2–3 seconds to notice.)
Again knowing you don't have to do anything about them,
Just notice what you are experiencing.

(Give them 2–3 seconds to notice.)
And when you feel ready,
You can bring your awareness back into the room,
And open your eyes.

Self Awareness

Debra A. Littrell
Transformative Spirit, LLC

Somatic & Energetic Resourcing™

Self Awareness—Simple Homework

Do the **Self Awareness** activity four times a day. Fill in the date, day of the week, the time of day you completed each practice session, and note what sensations, emotions and thought qualities you experienced during the activity.

Bring this sheet back with you to your next session.

Date:	Day of the Week:
Time	Sensations, Emotions & Thought Qualities You Experienced

Date:	Day of the Week:
Time	Sensations, Emotions & Thought Qualities You Experienced

Date:	Day of the Week:
Time	Sensations, Emotions & Thought Qualities You Experienced

© Copyright 2013 Debra Littrell All Rights Reserved. You may make copies to use in your own practice with your clients only. Otherwise this material cannot be altered, copied, or translated without the express, written permission of Debra A. Littrell.

Figure 2: Self Awareness—Simple
Page 1 of 2

Next Step: Self Awareness—Integrative

If your client can easily name sensations, emotions and thought qualities, in the next session you can move to ***Self Awareness—Integrative***. The difference is, now you are asking them to notice how their thinking may be affecting their emotions and body. Your client may already have developed the ability to witness themselves. Now they will be able to develop an ability to "learn their own language." Now they will be able to learn when things are right for them and take authentic action. Encourage them to do "experiments". What signals do they get, what happens when they listen to their innate signals, as opposed to what happens when they choose against their innate signals. For clients who are already skilled at witnessing themselves, you can move to the integrative grounding exercises right away. Be careful here. I have had many clients who are very active in Yoga, Pilates, and other physical activities who are not connected. They do the activities but they are not fully present in the activities. So test it out anyway.

The goal is for your clients to be Self aware 24 hours a day, 7 days a week so they will be in charge of their life.

The scripts are designed with neutral language. My work with negative and positive cognitions in EMDR Therapy taught me how much of an influence words have on what people perceive. This awareness further expanded when I took Conscious Language Courses and became a Language of Mastery Instructor with Mastery Systems. Therapists often contaminate these exercises with their own bias. Stay with the script to remain neutral. Only add a range of examples of emotions or sensations or thought qualities if your client is unable to come up with words to describe their experiences.

Somatic & Energetic Resourcing

Self Awareness—Integrative (Script)

I invite you to close your eyes.

Scan your body.

Noticing what physical sensations are present.

Notice what areas are comfortable & what areas are other than comfortable.

(Give them 2–3 seconds to notice.)

Turning your awareness to areas that are other than comfortable,

Notice what sensations tell you this is other than comfort.

Too hot, too cold,

Is there too much pressure or tightness,

Or, is there pain?

And if there is pain,

notice the quality of the pain.

Sharp, Dull, Burning, Constant, Or does it come and go.

(Give them 2–3 seconds to notice.)

Knowing you don't have to do anything about this, just notice what you are experiencing.

(Give them 2–3 seconds to notice.)

And now turning your awareness to areas of your body where you are experiencing comfort, or where you at least feel neutral,

Notice what sensations tell you this is comfort or neutrality.

Self Awareness

Noticing temperature,
How light or dense each area might be,
How loose or firm your muscles are,
How relaxed each area is.
    (Give them 2–3 seconds to notice.)

Just taking a moment to enjoy your more comfortable or neutral sensations.
    (Give them 2–3 seconds to notice.)

And now I invite you to turn your awareness to your emotions.
Noticing what emotions are present.
Noticing if you are experiencing more than one emotion.
And if there is more than one,
Notice if they are similar or congruent,
Or if they are opposites or incongruent.
    (Give them 2–3 seconds to notice.)

Again knowing you don't have to do anything about them,
Just notice what you are experiencing.
    (Give them 2–3 seconds to notice.)

And notice how your emotions may be affecting your physical body.
    (Give them 2–3 seconds to notice.)

Somatic & Energetic Resourcing

And now turning your awareness to your thinking,
You can notice what you are thinking.
But more importantly notice the quality of your thoughts.
Are they fast or slow or evenly paced,
Do they dart around,
or are they still.
> *(Give them 2–3 seconds to notice.)*

And noticing if they are about the past or the future,
Or are they right here in present time.
> *(Give them 2–3 seconds to notice.)*

Again knowing you do not have to do anything about them,
Just notice what you are experiencing.
> *(Give them 2–3 seconds to notice.)*

And, notice how your body & your emotions are being affected by your thinking.
> *(Give them 2–3 seconds to notice.)*

When you feel ready,
You can bring your awareness back into the room,
And open your eyes.

Self Awareness

Somatic & Energetic Resourcing™

Self Awareness—Integrative Homework

Do the **Self Awareness** activity four times a day. Fill in the date, day of the week, and then note the time of day you completed each **Self Awareness** practice session.

Bring this sheet back with you to your next session.

Date:							
Day of Week:							
Morning Time:							
Lunch Time:							
Dinner Time:							
Bedtime:							

Date:							
Day of Week:							
Morning Time:							
Lunch Time:							
Dinner Time:							
Bedtime:							

© Copyright 2013 Debra Littrell All Rights Reserved. You may make copies to use in your own practice with your clients only. Otherwise this material cannot be altered, copied, or translated without the express, written permission of Debra A. Littrell.

Figure 3: *Self Awareness—Integrative*
Page 1 of 1

Prescription

The prescription for ***Self Awareness*** is for them to practice it a minimum of 4 times a day. I suggest they link it with routine in their lives, e.g., when they wake in the morning before they get up, at lunch, at dinner and before they go to sleep at night. This pattern disrupts going through the day unconsciously, and brings more Self awareness throughout the day. Have them write down the date and times of day they practiced and bring this information into the next session. If they are having trouble complying, make sure they do the assigned activities in your office each session. For clients who are having trouble identifying sensations and emotions, have them jot down what they experienced during their ***Self awareness*** activity. There are CDs and MP3 downloads available through my retail website, transformativeproductions.com. I recorded them for those clients who are having difficulty doing this on their own.

How Long Does It Take?

The ***Self awareness*** practice on the CD is about 10 minutes long, and is self-soothing as well. As clients become more proficient at doing ***Self awareness*** they do not have to use the guided tools any longer. Some clients choose to use it once a day because the guided tools remind them of what to look for and they do briefer check-ins with themselves during the other times that day. Eventually clients report being more Self aware in every moment. And, some have reported some major changes in their lives just with more awareness.

Once a client gets proficient at Self awareness it only takes a few seconds to do the check-in.

Self Awareness

What Am I Assessing When I Do This Activity with My Clients?

When I do *Self Awareness* Activities they tell me:

- Can my client name a sensation? (primitive brain function, possible dissociation)
- Can they name emotions? (primitive brain function, possible dissociation)
- Are they giving me clear, accurate feedback?
- Are they trying to look for what I want?
- Are they able to stay connected with Self while in conversation with me? (dual focus)
- If they do not have the resource, does it begin to develop as they repeat the activities?
- Do these resources begin to spontaneously show up in their daily life?
- Do they get overwhelmed when they are connected with Self?
- Do they begin to report that they are becoming Self aware more often in their daily life?
- Do they develop the capacity to be Self aware most of the time during their daily life?
- What shows up differently in the choices they make when they are more Self aware in their daily life?

Chapter 8
Reconnecting to Innate Signals Within

Now that your client has some experience of identifying physical, emotional and cognitive signals, you can move into another awareness activity that helps them see how their thoughts and beliefs, reference points, definitions, etc. are creating their reality, and in many cases their suffering. Here is another activity where they can watch how their body, emotions, and cognitive qualities communicate with them.

In my early days facilitating for the EMDR Institute, while Francine Shapiro, Ph.D. was still teaching, she used to do an exercise in the training to demonstrate how people's physiology responded to their thoughts. She had them notice what occurred when she repeated the word "no" several times. She then had them do the same with the word "yes". Participants would share how their physiology would become contracted with the repeated no, and expanded with the yes. When I attended an introduction to the Hakomi Method the presenter did an exercise very similar to this. I found the statements she used very helpful in demonstrating how we have different responses to different viewpoints, so I have included them in this program. You can use any statements you wish, but these statements give you and your clients important informa-

Somatic & Energetic Resourcing

tion about what internal resources they may or may not have, while learning how their innate wisdom communicates with them.

This activity can also be an excellent opportunity for you to see if they are able to just witness and learn from what shows up, or if they disconnect from their innate signals and go up into their head to try to figure out what is going on, what you as their therapist are looking for, what this is all about, what this has to do with anything, and so on.

Notice as I made that list, did you go up in your head? If you did, that is a very important key for you. Especially for those of you who are energetically or somatically sensitive. When your client speaks from their thinking, instead of their being, you may go into your head just as they do. You are perceiving what is going on with them. Maybe even entraining with them. Be aware of your experience, trusting what you experience, using it to help your client reconnect, and making sure you reconnect without getting caught up in their disconnection.

This activity is also a precursor to:

1. Becoming aware of what is True for them.
2. Having more awareness of how their thinking points to how things are showing up in their world.
3. Interrupting their disconnection from Self when they get caught up in content during the session.
4. Both you and your client getting out of the content and into tools for changing the limitations. You can repeat this activity with them and use different words, just to give them more opportunity to discover how their innate Truth communicates with them.

Reconnecting to Innate Signals Within

After you have done this activity with them, you can interrupt them periodically when they are talking and ask them what signals their body, emotions and thought qualities are giving them as they talk. This integrates Self awareness into every session. It disrupts the disconnected-from-Self autopilot and assists them (1) to become more aware of how often and easily they become disconnected with themSelves, and (2) to perceive how their innate signals are always present, and how they may be missing them.

It also assists you in staying out of the content, and seeing how often you entrain to their disconnection.

This is a very valuable tool. I have had many clients who have made numerous spontaneous shifts in their awareness levels and their choices, just by having someone interrupt their unconscious autopilot once a week, and ask, "What are you noticing physically, emotionally, and cognitively, as you have been talking?"

Somatic & Energetic Resourcing

Reconnecting to Innate Signals Within (Script)

I invite you to close your eyes.   *(Wait 5 seconds)*

Scan your body from head to toe.   *(Wait 5 or 10 seconds)*

Notice what physical sensations you are experiencing.   *(Wait 5 seconds)*

Notice what emotions you are experiencing.   *(Wait 5 seconds)*

Notice what your thinking is doing.   *(Wait 5 seconds)*

You don't have to do anything about any of this, just notice. *(Wait 5 seconds)*

Now I am going to make three different statements and I would like you to notice what changes physically, emotionally and cognitively, when you hear them.

I invite you to notice what happens when you hear the words, You are welcome here.   *(Wait a couple of seconds)*

You are welcome here.   *(Wait 5–10 seconds)*

Now I will move to the next statement.

I invite you to notice what happens when you hear the words, You are safe here.   *(Wait a couple of seconds)*

You are safe here.   *(Wait 5–10 seconds)*

Now I will move to the last statement.

Reconnecting to Innate Signals Within

I invite you to notice what happens when you hear the words,

Your life is your own.   *(Wait a couple of seconds)*

Your life is your own.   *(Wait 5–10 seconds)*

When you are ready you can open your eyes and bring your awareness back into the room.

What Am I Assessing When I Do This Activity with My Clients?

When I do *Self Awareness* Activities they tell me:

- Can my client name a sensation? (primitive brain function, possible dissociation)
- Can they name emotions? (primitive brain function, possible dissociation)
- Are they giving me clear, accurate feedback?
- Are they trying to look for what I want?
- Are they able to stay connected with Self while in conversation with me? (dual focus)
- If they do not have the resource, does it begin to develop as they repeat the activities?
- Do these resources begin to spontaneously show up in their daily life?
- Do they get overwhelmed when they are connected with Self?
- Do they begin to report that they are becoming Self aware more often in their daily life?
- Do they develop the capacity to be Self aware most of the time during their daily life?
- What shows up differently in the choices they make when they are more Self aware in their daily life?

Chapter 9
Testing Safety & Relationship

One of the things I noticed over the years is many people create such adaptations to live in the world that it can be difficult to tell what is really going on. When I was preparing people for the reprocessing phases of EMDR Therapy I found that how they presented in session, what they said, did not match what would show up when we got to the resourcing activities. They appeared to be able to connect with me but when it came to creating safe places, many could not do so, and all sorts of interesting behaviors showed up.

I would discover they were trying to please me. They were not giving me clear information on what they were experiencing so I could not guide them accurately. They were trying to figure out what construct I was operating from, and trying to fit into it. Many did not have an internal sense of safety. They always measured safety by what was going on externally. They were not choosing what worked for them. These behaviors are always indicators of early developmental trauma, so they will have no idea how to even communicate this with you. It is just how it has always been. And, they are really bright people who have really good adaptation skills.

Somatic & Energetic Resourcing

The good news is, people are adaptable, and the bad news is, people are adaptable.

So I created this activity as a way for both myself and my client to discover where our relationship really stood and how much safety they had in their own system. The other benefit that showed up was that the pendulation involved created more core resource for my clients. This has been an eye-opening experience for my clients. Their awareness level often expands exponentially.

This activity allows you and your client to discover together:

1. Your ability to communicate subtle details with each other.
2. Whether your client feels safe sharing exactly what they are experiencing.
3. Whether your client thinks there is a right way to do things.
4. How safe your client feels with visual contact with you.
5. Whether there are boundary issues to address further on.
6. Your clients' ability to choose.
7. Whether your clients are trying to please you.

Now that your client has already been practicing **Self awareness**, both in session with you, and on their own between sessions, this **Testing Safety and Relationship** activity can be used. Safety and relationship are crucial for any form of treatment, especially for any kind of trauma work. You rely on your client to give you accurate information of their experience so you can guide them appropriately. Clients who withhold information to please you, or who think there is a right answer, or who are suspicious in nature, can interfere with efficacy of treatment. They can get themselves in very difficult situations in trauma work because they have not formed a sense of safety with you. Will they allow you to support them? If not, they have more work to do before trauma work can commence.

When to Use Testing Safety & Relationship

To be prudent, you can use this activity after *Self awareness* activities with every client. *Self awareness* is a prerequisite so they can subtly track their experience in this activity. If you can clearly assess that a client has good inter-relational skills, can report clearly, feels safe, and has a history of good therapeutic relationships with other therapists, you may skip this activity. If you find your client is having difficulty with containment or grounding activities, it is time to do this activity.

What You as the Therapist Must Do to Be Successful

When doing this or any somatic resourcing activity these elements are crucial:

1. You are in a neutral state of witnessing to support your client in developing a neutral state of witnessing themselves.
2. You avoid interpretations and encourage your client to learn their own language, what their physical, emotional and cognitive signals are telling them.
3. They are in charge. If they are uncomfortable or have to explore what they are experiencing, or what words

match what they are experiencing, you must give them the opportunity to do so in a safe and patient environment.

Yes, this is an artificial experience, and others in their lives will not be willing to give them this much leniency. They must have a safe place to explore and learn about themSelves and their defensive reactions with others, or their need to control others. With more Self awareness and sense of learning what is right for them, they begin to develop an ability to speak up, get out of problem situations, or be more direct, rather than having to manipulate.

This is very delicate work. It is very important that you go slow and allow your client the time to notice what is occurring for them. In some cases you will be working with very early developmental issues, from a time before verbal communication was developed. ***It is very important that you give your client the encouragement to "take their time to allow the words that match that experience to float up to their mind."***

When there has been preverbal wounding people will have the experience of what occurred, somatically, emotionally and energetically, but will have no words for it. If you give them a great deal of time and space the words will show up that match what they are experiencing. But it is important they allow the words to float up, and not for them to figure out what the words are. If they go up into their heads and start trying to make sense of it they will have disconnected from the "felt sense" of the experience, and the opportunity for changing things will be lost. You are looking to create a bridge, not be technical, rational, or make sense of it.

Testing Safety & Relationship

Exercise

If at any time your client becomes agitated or overwhelmed, ask them what they would like you to do. This demonstrates your willingness to honor what works for them, and helps them realize they can choose what works for them.

Go slow, watch for subtle signals.

1. Start with facing your client directly and ask them to check in with themselves and let you know what they are experiencing. What physical, emotional and cognitive signals are they experiencing? Is this comfortable or not?

2. Then tell them you will be turning your chair slightly off to the side. Turn your chair slightly off to one side so your body is at an angle to them, and still look directly at them. Again ask them to check in with themselves and tell you what they are experiencing, comfortable or not, and what physical, emotional and cognitive signals they are noticing.

3. Then tell them you will be turning your chair slightly off to the other side. Turn your chair slightly off to the other side, still looking at them directly. Ask them to check in with themselves and report their experience, physically, emotionally and cognitively.

4. Then tell them you will be turning your chair all the way around. Turn your chair completely around and face completely away from them, and ask what they are experiencing physically, emotionally and cognitively.

5. End the activity by asking them which position works best for them to continue the rest of the session from. Turn your chair to that position.

6. Be willing to change again if they ask you during the rest of the session.

Things to Be Aware Of

Some people are very uncomfortable with direct-facing contact. They may become overwhelmed, moving into a fight-or-flight response. Some are more comfortable off to one side or the other, some are not. These are all indications of where they guard or wall themselves off, to be addressed later on. For right now you are exploring. If they are very defended during this activity, and have difficulty communicating with you about what they are experiencing, your initial work will be about safety. Sometimes memories associated with where they feel exposed or walled-off show up. Add them to your target list for clearing limitations.

Sometimes having your client experience you directly facing them, then off to the side, then directly facing them, then off to the side, a number of times will decrease their discomfort with direct-facing contact. Some of this can have a desensitizing effect because they are able to slowly explore, discover and be empowered to say how they feel, and be respected by you.

For clients who are most comfortable when you face fully away, there is a major issue with safe contact with others. If you have already done a thorough developmental history you will already know where this originates. There may be in-utero trauma or stress that occurred, or early childhood neglect, abandonment or trauma. Or major traumatic events as an adult. Allowing your client to be in charge and going between facing fully away and then directly facing them, can help to repair their ability to communicate what is true for them, and choose what works.

Testing Safety & Relationship

Sometimes you will see them feel both relieved when you turn away, and abandoned at the same time. Again going back and forth between direct-facing contact and fully facing away, with them choosing when you move to each, repairs their experience. This is great for building trust and good communication between you and your client.

Many clients go through life hyper-vigilant all of the time, forcing themselves to be in contact because it is socially acceptable. This takes an enormous amount of energy to do all day, every day. This means they are in a chronic state of fight-or-flight. They are unable to use their higher reasoning skills. Their immune system may become, or will already be, depleted. Creating an internal sense of safety allows them to live in a parasympathetic state.

Sometimes you will see clients who are resistant to experiencing the back-and-forth. Always offer this activity as an experiment, so they can gather more information about themselves, and make sure they know they can always have you move to a more comfortable position for them. If they feel very unsafe, and their physical, emotional and cognitive signals are saying "no", then honor what is right for them. Then ask them what they experience, now that they shared with you what is right for them, and you listened and respected them.

Sometimes clients say, "other people will not do this for me." I tell my clients that here is a place they get to explore what is right for them and learn more about themSelves. When are they listening to themSelves and setting limits with others, or telling others the Truth? When are they not listening to themSelves, or not setting limits or telling others what is True for them? What do they experience physically, emotionally and cognitively when they do either?

The interesting thing is, often they come back the next session able to do the same activity with ease. The resource was built and showed up organically just from what we did in the office.

Testing Safety and Relationship is a delicate tool. There are many choice points that you will encounter. If you are unsure of this activity, I would recommend setting up consultation time with me to practice and learn some of the subtleties.

What Am I Assessing When I Do This Activity with My Clients?

Testing Safety and Relationship helps me identify:

- What pace truly works for them.
- If they are willing to truthfully communicate what they are experiencing, including the subtle details. Whether your client feels safe sharing exactly what they are experiencing.
- How safe your client feels with visual contact with you.
- If they are willing to truthfully tell you what works best for them.
- If they try to override Truth for them by telling you what they "think" the right thing "should" be.
- Whether there are boundary issues to address further on.
- Your clients' ability to choose.
- Whether your clients are trying to please you.

Chapter 10
Containment

Some clients are flooded easily by their emotions, and some are easily overwhelmed by sensory stimuli. Some have difficulty sensing what they are feeling physically or emotionally. If the more primitive parts of their brain are not fully developed or have been injured, people will have these issues. If they have suffered trauma, these symptoms will show up as well. The question is, What is causing the overwhelm or flooding? Using containment activities can help clients manage and decrease overwhelm or flooding. If containment helps, and works very well, the flooding or overwhelm is probably only from emotional or psychological aspects of trauma. If containment does not work, or only seems to help a little, there is probably a neurological problem, and referral for further assessment would be appropriate.

I learned these containment activities from Ditte Marcher, the daughter of Lisbeth Marcher who developed the Bodynamic program. I hosted her in the Seattle area to do some introductory courses, including one for mental health professionals and emergency service personnel. Ditte had done a great deal of work in war zones through the United Nations.

For clients who have difficulty staying connected with their body, or sensing their somatic signals, containment can help them have a "felt sense" of themselves. However, there can still be a neurological underpinning that requires correction.

Timing of teaching containment is at your discretion. If your client floods with **Self awareness** activities, containment is appropriate to teach immediately afterwards. If they flood during any of these activities, it is appropriate to teach them containment. If you are using the **Testing Safety and Relationship** activity and your client is feeling overwhelmed or unsafe, teach them **Containment**.

If **Containment** activities work very well, your client probably has the neurological foundation to handle strong emotions. If they do not work well, I recommend that the client be evaluated by a Neurological Reorganizational Therapy Specialist. There are only a handful of them around the US. You can contact Bette Lamont at neurologicalreorganization.com to see if she does evaluations in your area, or who she could refer you to. This work is very effective in repairing neurological problems. Although Occupational Therapists do some of this work, they do not include all of the developmental movements that may be required to repair the most primitive deficits. This is why I recommend Neurological Reorganizational Therapy Specialists.

Muscles on the outside of our arms and legs are containment muscles. Engaging them will cut emotional overwhelm. People report still feeling emotion but are not overwhelmed; they can think more clearly, and act accordingly.

In many cases, clients have difficulty staying connected with their body, sensing themselves. **Containment** helps them be

Containment

able to feel. In these cases there is definitely a neurological underpinning requiring evaluation and treatment.

Containment activities are too difficult to describe in a script. You will have to learn them in class demonstrations, class practice, in your own experience as a client, or in a consultation session. If you wish to learn the experiential part of this you can contact me through my website: transformativespirit.com and set up an appointment to learn this. It does not take very long and can be done via video conferencing.

Somatic & Energetic Resourcing

What Am I Assessing When I Do This Activity with My Clients?

When they do **Containment**, I am looking for:

If they have been unable to sense Self:

- Are they able to sense emotions and physical sensations?
- Are they able to put words to the emotions and sensations they are experiencing?

If they flood easily:

- Does the intensity of the emotions and/or sensations decrease?
- If so, are they able to continue to work using containment?

For both:

- Which of the three activities work best for them?
- Are they willing to practice all three?
- Do they use it in between sessions?

Chapter 11
Eyes Open/Eyes Closed

One of the things I noticed in my practice was that with their eyes closed people could feel connected with themselves and really experience the peace and bliss they are. Then when they would open their eyes they would lose their connection with self, and become increasingly disturbed the more they spoke. I have seen and experienced this with meditation as well. The idea behind meditation is that people become increasingly connected with their authentic Self, and the source from which they were created, and can then live more from their innate wisdom in their lives. Except I was not seeing this occur very much, or at all consistently. So I began to ask, What could I create that would assist people in becoming more aware of when they are connected, and when they disconnect? I developed the Eyes Open/Eyes Closed activity as a way for my clients and myself to discover how much they were able to stay connected to themSelves, while in interaction with others and the world around them.

After doing Self awareness activities with them so they were able to notice more subtle signals, I began having them explore what occurred with their connection with Self when their eyes were closed, and what changed when they were open. It was pretty eye-opening. Many reported they literally felt like they jumped out of their own body and were over there on the wall, or in my lap if they were looking at me. And I could feel that energetic pressure when they were in my space.

I have found that back-and-forth pendulation is very helpful in titrating activation, just like in previous activities I have already described. So I added it to Eyes Open/Eyes Closed. Over time people were able to stay connected to themSelves, and still see the object they were looking at. Rather than being withdrawn inside their body (disconnected from the world around them), or completely disconnected from their body, they were able to be in contact with both. This is another tool for developing the capacity to observe Self.

After doing this with inanimate objects we started adding in looking at me. And once again they would go to disconnection. They could stay connected to Self when looking at inanimate objects but not when in contact with people. So we did the same activity and pendulated back and forth until they were able to stay in contact with Self and with me simultaneously. An ease with staying connected with Self while in contact with others developed over time. This also strengthened their own authentic "felt-sense" of Self as opposed to ego.

This again is an activity that may need to be practiced in the office a number of times to build their capacity. Your clients can do it for themselves as well during the week. It will be easier for them to do it with inanimate objects on their own. Eventually they will get comfortable with practicing the activity with people as they go throughout their day. This really empowers them, over time, to stay centered within themselves while around others.

Activity

Have your client sit somewhere in your office where, when they open their eyes, they are looking at something neutral, ie: the wall, a plant, a bookshelf.

Invite them to close their eyes.

Have them do a couple of slow breaths.

Invite them to notice their body, then their emotions, and then their thought quality.

Remind them they do not have to do anything about this, just notice.

Invite them to focus on the core of their body, perhaps their heart, to notice the central core of their body up and down their spine.

Once they feel centered in their core, invite them to open their eyes.

Ask them what they notice. Did they stay connected to their core, or jump across the room?

Reassure them that whatever occurred is just fine. The two of you are just noticing what occurs.

If they did jump across the room energetically, ask them to pull themselves back into their body, their core, with their eyes still open.

If they are unable to do so, have them close their eyes and refocus on their heart, their center, their core, and to let you know when they are centered in themselves again.

Somatic & Energetic Resourcing

Now ask them to open their eyes again, and see what they notice.

Then ask them to share with you what occurred.

If they jumped across the room again, ask them if they can pull their energy back into their core with their eyes open.

If they cannot, have them close their eyes and re-center.

Repeat this process until they are able to stay connected with themSelves when they open their eyes. For those who just can't get it the first time, that is OK. The practice over time will allow them to stay connected.

Most people will begin to find it easier and easier to either be able to pull themselves back to center with their eyes open, or stay centered when they open their eyes. The more they practice, the easier it gets.

After they can do it with inanimate objects pretty easily, you can move to the next phase. Have them do the same activity, but this time they are facing you and when they open their eyes they will be looking at you. This takes it to the next level of being able to stay present with themSelves while in the presence of others. They begin to develop more and more confidence and stay with what is True for them.

Eyes Open/Eyes Closed

Assignment

For those who have difficulty staying connected, assign them to do this four times a day. To start out practicing with inanimate objects and eventually move to people. It only has to take a couple of minutes to practice.

Make sure to practice in each session until they get it as well. They may require your facilitation for awhile.

What Am I Assessing When I Do This Activity with My Clients?

Eyes Open/Eyes Closed tells me:

- Are they able to center themselves with their eyes closed?
- Are they able to stay in contact with Self when they open their eyes, in contact with the outside world?
- Are they looking to the outside world for cues on what they should do or be?
- Can they dual focus?
- Can they dual focus during trauma work? Particularly during the Desensitization Phase of EMDR Therapy.
- Can they stay present with Self during trauma work?

Chapter 12
Creating a "Felt Sense" of Resource

"Felt sense" resourcing is very different than imagining. Once I added "felt sense" resourcing, I found clients could really receive and step into the resource. When I used imaginal resourcing on its own, I did not find the resource was really accessible to clients in their daily lives. It appeared to be more of a fantasy than a fully embodied resource.

There are a number of ways to strengthen a client's "felt sense" of any resource. For instance, once they have the "felt sense" of being connected to Self, not the imagination of it, they can notice the sensations and emotions they are presently experiencing when they are fully connected to Self. You can use very slow bilateral taps to reinforce their connection with Self. And, your clients can do this themselves in your office.

There are a couple of other tools you can use. One is called Cook's Hook Up, and the other is Temporal Hold. If you already know these methods you can use them. If not, you can research them and use them. They are easy to learn. For those of you who are already EMDR Therapy trained, you will already have learned the slow bilateral stimulation for resource development in the Basic Training. If not, I recommend researching how they are done and adding these somatic activities to your resourcing with clients.

I find having more than one option is very helpful. Some clients get overwhelmed with bilateral stimulation. Some get very distracted moving into Cook's Hook Up. The Temporal Hold is really easy to use and is not distracting. I suggest you learn these techniques, let your client experience all three, and choose what works best for them. Let them experience which is the easiest, the least distracting and really strengthens the "felt sense" of the resource you are installing. You do not have to learn the whole methodology of each, just the basics. For those of you who are EMDR Therapy trained you can include the resourcing protocol. If you would like help with this, you can contact me and schedule a time to go through the activities with me to get the "felt sense" of how to use each one yourself.

Creating a "Felt Sense" of Resource

Strengthening the "Felt Sense" of Resource

To create the "felt sense" of the resource, have your client do any of the resourcing activities in this program. Once your client has the "felt sense" of the resource you are working with (safety, connected, centered, or supported) have them describe what they experience—sensations and emotions.

Have them do Cook's Hook Up or the Temporal Hold. Or, if you are EMDR Therapy trained, do the installation using taps or EMs.

Ask them what else they notice now.

If they describe a deeper, stronger sense of being grounded, centered, supported, or they experience more calm or peace, have them do Cook's Hook Up or the Temporal Hold. Or, if you are EMDR Therapy trained, do the installation using taps or EMs.

Again, ask them what else they notice.

If they describe a deeper, stronger sense of being grounded, centered, supported, or they experience more calm or peace, have them do Cook's Hook Up or the Temporal Hold. Or, if you are EMDR Therapy trained, do the installation using taps or EMs.

What do they notice?

What sensations do they notice in their body?

What sensations go with that sense of being safe, grounded, centered, supported?

Somatic & Energetic Resourcing

To strengthen what they are experiencing have them do Cook's Hook Up or the Temporal Hold. Or, if you are EMDR Therapy trained, do the installation using taps or EMs.

Continue to strengthen their "felt sense" of the resource until they report what they are experiencing stays the same.

Chapter 13
Recognizing Truth

How do you know what is True for your client? How does your client know what is True for them? Authentically True, not ego true. Authentically True, not left brain limitation true. Have you been operating from external reference points to determine what is right or wrong for your client? Is your client operating from choosing, based on external sources, what is right or wrong? What if both of you could explore what is True for your client? What if you were just a facilitator assisting your client in discovering how to be aware of (1) what is True for them, Authentically True, and (2) when they are choosing *for* themSelves or *against* themSelves? What if people's symptoms went away when they lived and chose based on what is Authentically True for them?

So how do you do that? First you have to get out of your head, out of what you think or have been told is right or good for clients. If you are operating from mental construct, instead of awareness of Truth, you will be learning right along with them. Learning how to step into awareness of Truth and choosing from Truth. Being aware of Truth is completely different from thinking. As you become more somatically and energetically aware, facilitation of clients will become very easy. As you clear out your dependence on thinking and mental concepts, and get out of the story and content, a wealth of information will become available. By creating activities with your client, you will both be learning and practicing how to be aware of what is True.

Now that you and your client have already practiced and developed Self awareness, and learned to be present, you can move on to being aware of Truth. You and your client will both have to have the capacity to sense your somatic, and eventually energetic, signals. The ability to sense physical, emotional, cognitive and energetic signals has to be in place to move to this next phase. Being present enough to notice those signals is also imperative. Are you ready? Here we go.

Truth vs. Limitation

What I have said to people, since my body-centered training, is, "Your body and emotions will give you information about what works for you and what does not. You have to learn your own language. How your innate wisdom communicates with you."

Anything that makes us feel heavy or weak, contracted, sad, angry, limited, stuck, etc., is a clear indicator that there is some sort of lie or limitation operating. As I mentioned earlier, and often describe to clients, if you watch young kids you will see a good example of what our innate authentic state looks like. (Assuming the kids have not already suffered from trauma or neglect.) Little kids are full of energy and joy. They laugh and play. They are curious about the world. Every day is a new adventure. They tend to include everyone, and it does not make much sense to them why the big people cannot get

Recognizing Truth

along. They have not yet formed beliefs and rules that cause separation and limitation.

If they do get upset, it tends to be over fairly quickly and they do not tend to hold grudges. The energy in their system just flows. They are good examples of what our Authenticity looks like.

There are few adults in the world who function this way. The most publicly known is the Dalai Lama. He is known to smile and laugh, and be much like a little kid all of the time. People feel good just being around him. There are other less well-known people also in the public eye, such as Eckhart Tolle, Gregg Braden, and Howard Martin. They just have an ease and joy about them. All of these people see the value in others, and have a way of conversing with the innate Truth in those they are speaking with. They see past the egoic limitations and engage with the Authentic Self in others. People have a sense of being valued by them, even in brief conversations.

Returning home, Living Authentically™, is about returning to this natural state. Giving up the identifications, labels, choices, roles, jobs, relationships, that cut this life-giving flow to us. And, choosing things that are in alignment with who we are so we live in joy, instead of burden and obligation.

We already set the stage earlier with the activity in Chapter 8, Reconnecting to the Innate Signals Within, where your clients had the opportunity to notice the physical, emotional and cognitive reactions to three specific statements. Now we are taking this to another level, to notice what is True for them and what is not.

Somatic & Energetic Resourcing

Anything that makes us feel heavy, weak, contracted, limited, sad, guilty, etc., indicates there is some sort of lie or limitation operating that is cutting off our natural flow of energy. So a lie or limitation will always make us feel heavy, weak, contracted, less aware, emotionally upset. When we are Living Authentically™, from our innate Truth, we feel lighter, stronger, more expansive, joyful. There is a sense of ease.

When we experience heaviness, weakness, contraction, fear, anger, guilt, physical pain, our innate wisdom is communicating with us. We get very clear signals when we are off the mark, when we have strayed from Truth, when what we are choosing is not working for us. The heaviness or weakness comes from cutting off the energy flow in our systems. Our job is to facilitate clients to (1) perceive these signals, (2) trust their innate Truth instead of looking to external sources, or shutting up the Truth, and (3) choose what will restore them to joy.

For some clients this will be easy; they have some previous experience with living at ease. For others you will have to create experiences in your office, since the amount of repetitive trauma in their lives may have interfered with them having much in the way of joyful experiences. For some it will be a steep learning curve, because they have developed a protective mechanism to take anything joyful away from themselves before anyone else does.

As your client discovers what limitations, beliefs and lies they may be operating from, you can note them and use whatever tools you use for clearing or desensitizing the limitations. As I mentioned earlier, these somatic and energetic activities will flush out targets to clear or desensitize as you go through them. Create a list so you can systematically clear them when you get to that phase of treatment.

Activity for Identifying Truth vs Limitation

So how can you test Truth vs lie or limitation? I like to start with the client's name. This is pretty obvious, so it is a good place for them to begin noticing how they respond physically, emotionally and energetically. Before you start, have them do a quick physical, emotional and energetic scan of how they are right now as a base line. Have them say, "My name is _____ (fill in their name)." Then ask them if they feel lighter, stronger, more expanded, or heavier, weaker, more contracted.

Then have them say, "My name is _____ (fill in a name that is not theirs)." Then ask them if they feel lighter, stronger, more expanded or heavier, weaker, more contracted. For most people this is very effective. Some have difficulty because they go into their head to figure things out. So ask a question, "Were you aware of your physical and emotional response, or did you go into your head and start thinking?" This is invaluable for them to see how their thinking gets in the way of awareness, of receiving the signals of the innate wisdom within, guiding them back to health. Just studying how their thinking derails them is very eye-opening.

Some people have difficulty with their names. Some have changed their names to something that does not resonate with them. Some have so many negative beliefs about themselves that they get a contracted response. Just be curious, and ask, "What is that?" (Without having to have an answer.)

Then you can move into other things to test. "I like _____." Light, stronger, more expanded? Or, heavy, weaker, more contracted?

Recognizing Truth

''I like _____ (insert something they do not like).'' Light, stronger, more expanded? Or heavy, weaker, more contracted?

"My favorite food is _____." Light, stronger, more expanded? Or, heavy, weaker, more contracted?

"My favorite food is   grass ." Light, stronger, more expanded? Or heavy, weaker, more contracted?

I like to put in some playful things to make it more fun. To get out of making it a big deal. To help them realize this is an innate capacity they already have, that they have shut off somewhere in their life.

Integrating Awareness of Truth in Sessions

Then you can move on to using this during a session. As they are talking, notice—do you feel light, more expanded? Or, heavy, more contracted? If you are feeling heavier or contracted, interrupt them and ask them to notice. Are they in their head or in their awareness? Do they feel light, strong, more expanded or heavy, weak, more contracted?

Doing these periodic interruptions throughout the session assists them in observing how aware or present they are, or are not. They become more aware of how their innate wisdom is communicating with them through their body, emotions and thought qualities. They learn to observe how they cut off their awareness, and how what is True is always available to them, but they miss it. Eventually, they become more aware of how being aware gives them more access to what is True, and the opportunity to choose it. As they progress in their awareness and ability to know Truth, they learn how they have been creating Self limitation, by not being aware.

The more they use this tool, the more they discover they can change anything by being aware of what is True for them and choosing based on what is True for them. Choosing against themselves in favor of mental computation, they talk themselves out of choosing Truth. The more you use this tool in session with them, the more you interrupt their unconscious patterns of not being aware all the time, and not listening to the innate signals that are always there for them.

I often ask people how many times they knew what was correct for them, but talked themselves out of it because _____ (there are many reasons and justifi-

Recognizing Truth

cations). There are always reasons why they choose against themSelves. Many people will totally defend why they have to choose against themSelves in favor of external obligations. Then the bottom line is, ARE THEY WILLING TO CHANGE THIS?

I have had some practitioners who go into a cynical point of view about the energetics of learning awareness, because they have a mental construct that energy work is "woo-woo". It really is not, it is very practical. Here is an example. I was teaching how to be aware of Truth to some of my EMDR Therapy consultees. They said this was a very different way to practice. And, asked how this related to EMDR Therapy. I asked them what they experienced in the training, physically and emotionally, when they were choosing a memory to target during the practicum. They named a variety of upsetting emotions and physical discomforts. Then I asked them, did that feel expansive or light, or contracted or heavy when they had those reactions. They all said they felt heavy. Then I asked what physical and emotional reactions they had when they completed clearing the targeted memory. They all reported positive emotions and more comfortable sensations. Then I asked if they felt expansive or contracted when they experienced those positive emotions and more comfortable sensations. All agreed they felt much lighter after they cleared the memory. They got it. We all feel lighter or more expansive once we give up the lies and limitations we carry around.

I have noticed over the years that when clients completely clear a limitation they perk up, get more energy, feel more at ease, have more peace, feel lighter. They often go bounding out of my office ready to play! I have noticed at other times, when we have worked on clearing an issue, although they have a more positive perspective, they are drained and tired at the end of the session. They usually report the next time we meet that a bunch of other stuff came up between sessions. So the target was not completely cleared. It may have looked clear from what they *said*, but total freedom from the issue was not showing up in their system, physical, emotional and cognitive. So I trust this now. If they are tired and drained, I am curious about what else is asking to change. If you are working on a EMDR Therapy Treatment Planning Worksheet there may be other memories on the list, not yet cleared, still affecting their system. If you don't use this kind of systematic approach, you just keep in mind there is something still dragging on their system, another self-limiting belief, memory, etc.

This Is Just the Beginning

This is just the foundation for becoming aware of Truth. It is a starting point. Once people get good at noticing light/more expanded and heavy/more contracted, they have to learn how to use questions to flush out more information to base their choices on. The biggest mistake people make is, going into assumption or conclusion that because something is heavy it is wrong, and they won't choose it. By asking their *Authentic Self* more questions, they get more awareness. For example: "Will a different configuration work?" "Now or in the future?" "Can I change it?" "How can I change it?" "In this location? Or, another?" "With this trainer? Or, another?" Then they have a bigger picture.

For instance, looking for a job. Would this job be fun and lucrative for me? Expansive or contracted? Contracted. Would this job in a different company be fun and lucrative for me? Expansive. So the job itself would be a contribution, but a different company would work, and the one they are looking at would not. Could be the supervisor won't work. It could be the culture of the company does not work. Could be the ethics of the company would not work. The energy will point to what we may not be able to pick up until actually working for the company. So when I notice contraction, I trust it and ask more questions. I don't have to discard the whole thing. Just ask my *Authentic Self* what would work. Where would it work? With whom will it work? In what location will it work? With which supervisor will it work? Yes, this takes developing a relationship with the Authentic Self, the innate wisdom within, and learning to trust it.

Sometimes things feel lighter or more expansive because clients have entrained to someone else's excitement. With more practice in noticing how the "felt sense" of Truth and lie or limitation feels in their system, or shows up somatically or energetically, clients learn to discern what is theirs, and what they are aware of that is someone else's. This gets more and more subtle the more they work with it.

What Am I Assessing When I Do This Activity with My Clients?

When I do **Truth vs. Lie or Limitation**, I am assessing:

- How do their innate signals communicate with them? Emotionally, physically, and/or energetically?
- How quickly do they develop this capacity?
- Do they choose what is True for themSelves, or against themSelves?
- Is their Self Awareness improving?
- Are there blocking beliefs or secondary gains showing up?
- Are they willing to connect with their innate Truth? What are the payoffs for not connecting?

Chapter 14
Is This Even Mine?

This is an excellent question to teach your clients to ask. "Is this even mine, or is it someone else's?" Often people make choices based on what they are aware of in others, rather than what is True for themSelves. Another interesting learning curve. Many people are very psychically aware and have never learned any tools for how to discern what is theirs and what is not, or how to use their awareness for them, instead of taking on other people's stuff and getting sick from it.

Everyone assumes the thoughts, feelings and emotions they are experiencing are theirs. Not necessarily true. And in most cases it is not. Around 48% of the population is energetically aware, and many have never had anyone 1) bring this to their awareness, 2) help them learn how to discern the difference between what is theirs and what they are aware of in others, or 3) learn how to handle what comes up that is not theirs.

I realize this is outside the typical practice of the mental health profession, but I cannot say that I have seen much training in the profession about identifying those who have energetic sensitivities. Nor has there been much in the way of research in what is different for them, or what works for them, es-

Somatic & Energetic Resourcing

pecially since many of the traditional tools do not work for them. They are often what are considered the "outliers" by researchers.

I have found that both those who are psychically and energetically sensitive and those who are not, will benefit from learning the subtleties of what is going on around them, and how their body and emotions can sense these subtleties. The benefits for those who are energetically aware are enormous. In some cases, just learning how aware they are, and how to use this awareness, has turned everything around for them in a very short period of time. Once they learn to consistently ask, "Is this even mine?", they can discern what is their issue, and what is not. What requires a response from them, and what does not. They learn how to use what they are perceiving in others to choose how to interact with them.

How many people are medicated because they are aware of everyone else's stuff and think it is theirs, but when they try to change it they cannot, because it is not theirs? How many people have been making up stories that there is something wrong with them because of what they are aware of in others? How many have received mental health diagnoses because they are aware of distress in others, and cannot change it because it is not theirs?

So this is one of the first tools I teach clients. Is this yours? If they feel lighter after that question, then they just dropped a bunch of stuff they have been carrying around that is not theirs, not them. That is why they feel lighter, more expansive, or a sense of relief. They just let go of what is not them.

I realize for some of you this is a completely foreign concept. For others of you this will make perfect sense. For those of

Is This Even Mine?

you who find this very foreign, I invite you to leave that pesky left brain behind and play with this new tool, and see what shows up. For those of you who are so relieved someone finally said it, play on!!!!

Ever notice when you walk into a room of people you don't know, who were arguing before you walked in, that the energy in the room is heavy? You feel the heaviness. Do you own it because you feel it? Do you go into thinking there is something wrong with you, even though you have not done anything yet or interacted with anyone yet? What if you did own it? How many stories would you make up in your head about yourself that were not true, that you began to use to define yourself? How would this alter your actions with others, your choices? But it was not about you, and you cannot change what is not yours. So how much would you then go into a downward spiral about what is wrong with you, that you cannot change?

For people who are psychically aware this occurs all of the time. Walking down the street, in a store, while driving, in a meeting, around friends or loved ones, etc. Once they learn to be aware of the difference between what is theirs and what they are noticing in others, much can change for them rather rapidly. A whole new world opens up for them. They stop taking on what is not theirs and they start choosing what does work for them. For some it can take awhile to learn this. And, it has to be the first question they ask themselves about everything, since they may have spent many years of their life in a pattern of taking on other people's thoughts, emotions and even physical sensations.

First teach them to ask, about every thought, every emotion, every physical sensation, "Is this even mine?" If they feel relief, just tell them to let go of it, send back what is not theirs (they cannot change it, it is not theirs). Support them in giving up the identification that it is theirs. Sometimes I run into people feeling they should fix it for others. This is often one of the major blocks to change. The thing is, by trying to fix it, they could actually cause more harm and delay the person in changing things for themselves. And, we can't fix other people's stuff. It does not work. So just let go of it, send it back. If someone asks for assistance and they are willing to receive help, then contribute without taking it on.

This is a very powerful tool. Along with the previous activity of identifying what is True and what is not, identifying what is theirs and what they are just perceiving in others, can be tremendously freeing. This one question, "Is this even mine?", can open up a whole new world. And, if you use it continually you will unveil more about how and what we take on from others for many years to come. It is amazing how much we can be aware of in others and in groups, that we have mis-identified as ours and then tried to change it, with no success. If we are identifying someone else's physical, emotional or thinking patterns as ours it will feel heavy, contracted. Because it is not True for us.

I have had many clients for whom this tool has created tremendous relief. And, it has opened up a whole new world of ease for them. Getting people in the habit of asking this question about everything, all of the time, is the learning curve.

As your client is talking in session and you notice the room feels heavier, or you are feeling more tired, or contracted, is

Is This Even Mine?

it yours or theirs? Let it go. Then ask them what they notice. Light or heavy? Expansive or contracted? Is it theirs, or did they buy it from someone else? See how much stuff we share with each other, and buy from each other, that we never even ask about?

Do this frequently during the session. Especially for really in-their-heads clients. They are so disconnected from Truth by being in the story and content in their heads that they will require frequent and repeated interventions, until they become more aware during sessions.

If you tend to be really in your head, this will be a big learning curve for you as well. You will get hooked into the content and the story, instead of doing interventions that will change things. The more you do experiential activities where both of you can notice the difference, the more impact you will have for change.

Assign your client to ask themselves, for every thought, for every emotion, and for every physical sensation, "Is this even mine?" I have had many clients avoid some pretty horrendous situations because they asked this question, and were able to bypass a great deal of suffering. I have had clients who were victims of sexual assault and had a general fear of everyone. Once they learned this tool they realized that they had picked up signals from attackers but thought there was something wrong with them. They then reported having similar feelings around new people they met and chose not to interact or form relationships. They chose not to go down that road again. They also reported the new relationships they were forming were more honest, supportive and joyful.

Somatic & Energetic Resourcing

What Am I Assessing When I Do This Activity with My Clients?

When I do Is This Even Mine?, I am assessing:

- Are they reading their physical and emotional signals?
- Are they able to perceive their energetic signals?
- Have they always been aware of their energetic signals, but did not know how to use that information? Or, used it in a way that was limiting their Self?
- Are they giving me clear and accurate feedback, or are they looking for what I want, or trying to please me?
- How quickly do they integrate this capacity?
- Do they use this tool in between sessions?

Chapter 15
Support in a Chair

There are many clients who have not experienced a sense of support in their lives. When you do a developmental history, look for what kind of support they experienced from their family growing up. Has there been anyone in their community who your client was able to receive some support from—teachers, coaches, friends' parents? Clients who have had little support will present with self-reliance, having difficulty allowing others to help or support them. You may also find those who cannot think of a place where they have ever felt safe. And, some who cannot even make up in their imagination a safe place for themselves. These people will be unable to take in support.

Support in a Chair activity is a way for them to begin to let support in. The support is being provided by a chair, an inanimate object, which has no motives. This provides them an opportunity to explore what it is like to take in support without high risk. Do this activity in your office with them each session, so they also receive support from you. Prescribe them this activity at least twice a day.

Somatic & Energetic Resourcing

The script is written in neutral language to focus on sensations, to allow your client's experience to unfold from what is True for them. Please refrain from inserting ideas, images, comparisons or concepts. This is a somatic activity, not imaginal. We are looking to develop their "felt sense" muscle, not their thinking muscle. Their thinking muscle is already overdeveloped and creating imbalance in the system.

If your client has difficulty doing this activity on their own, they can order the Somatic Resourcing 1, Mindfulness CD or MP3 I recorded, which has Mindfulness activities, as well as the Support in a Chair track. The Somatic Resourcing CDs were recorded for those clients who have difficulty doing the activities on their own. There is more information about the recordings on my Transformative Productions retail website at: transformativeproductions.com At the time of this publication there is a link on that page to purchase them.

Support in a Chair (Script)

I invite you to close your eyes.

Checking the bottoms of your feet.

Noticing how they connect to the floor. *(Wait 2–3 seconds.)*

Feel the floor support your feet, *(Wait 2–3 seconds.)*

Holding them in place. *(Wait 2–3 seconds.)*

Noticing how no effort on your part is required to be supported by the floor. *(Wait 2–3 seconds.)*

Now turning your awareness to your legs and sit bones,

Noticing how they connect to the surface beneath you. *(Wait 2–3 seconds.)*

Feeling how this surface holds you in place. *(Wait 2–3 seconds.)*

Feel the support of this surface. *(Wait 2–3 seconds.)*

Knowing you are not required to do anything to receive this support, *(Wait 2–3 seconds.)*

It is just there for you. *(Wait 2–3 seconds.)*

And turning your awareness to your back.

Notice how the surface behind you connects to your back. *(Wait 2–3 seconds.)*

Feel how it holds you in place. *(Wait 2–3 seconds.)*

Just enjoying your support. *(Wait 2–3 seconds.)*

And feeling your arms being held in place by the surface beneath them, *(Wait 2–3 seconds.)*

Somatic & Energetic Resourcing

Notice the support. *(Wait 2–3 seconds.)*

Again, notice how it takes no effort on your part to receive this support. *(Wait 2–3 seconds.)*

And noticing overall,
How your feet are held in place by the floor beneath them.
How your legs and your sit bones are supported by the surface beneath them.
And how your back is supported by the surface behind you. *(Wait 2–3 seconds.)*

Again noticing how you don't have to do anything to receive this support,
It is just there for you. *(Wait 2–3 seconds.)*
Taking a moment to enjoy. *(Wait 5–10 seconds.)*

And when you feel ready,
You can bring your awareness back into the room,
And open your eyes.

Support in a Chair

Somatic & Energetic Resourcing™

Support in a Chair Homework

Do the **Support in a Chair** activity twice a day. Fill in the date, day of the week and the time of day you completed each practice session, and note what you experienced during the activity.

Bring this sheet back with you to your next session.

Date:	Day of the Week:
Time	Sensations, Emotions & Thought Qualities you experienced

Date:	Day of the Week:
Time	Sensations, Emotions & Thought Qualities you experienced

Date:	Day of the Week:
Time	Sensations, Emotions & Thought Qualities you experienced

Date:	Day of the Week:
Time	Sensations, Emotions & Thought Qualities you experienced

© Copyright 2013 Debra Littrell All Rights Reserved. You may make copies to use in your own practice with your clients only. Otherwise this material cannot be altered, copied, or translated without the express, written permission of Debra A. Littrell.

Figure 4: Support in a Chair
Page 1 of 2

What Am I Assessing When I Do This Activity with My Clients?

The *Support In A Chair* activity helps me assess:

- Is my client able to receive support? This is an activity with an inanimate object, so if they cannot do this they may very well have difficulty feeling supported by people.
- Do they get over-stimulated by the idea of support?
- Do they have defense strategies that will default to negative if they have received support or a positive experience?

Chapter 16
Developmental Foundation of Connection with Self & Centering

Neural Pathway Development

When we are developing, all the developmental activities we do are about connection with our bodies, being embodied and creating neural pathways in our brains. When kids creep, crawl, cross-pattern, etc. they are creating massive amounts of connection in many areas; connection with their bodies and the earth, centering, sensory capacity, math skills, attention capacity, and more. When kids miss or are limited in these activities, it shows up in a variety of ways: lack of coordination, bumping into things, accident proneness, problems with impulse control, difficulty focusing, math and reading problems, being easily overwhelmed, unable to read social signals in others, and so on.

We actually refine our connections with body, earth, centering, and sensory capacity, at each age with a variety of different activities. It is always amazing to me how kids in all cultures spontaneously do the same activities in the same age ranges around the world. And they continue to do activities and even games, that are about developing more, as they get older.

Somatic & Energetic Resourcing

Unfortunately, we interfere with these natural activities in many ways. There are cultural limitations, social limitations, space limitations, etc. Some kids are kept off their bellies to creep and crawl because their family lives in a hut that has a dirt floor, and the parents do not want them in the dirt. In industrial nations kids are put in swings, walkers, play pens, and a variety of other contraptions to keep them out from under foot, to keep them quiet.

Did you know, when infants are on their bellies, and they hear or glimpse things in the periphery of their vision, their curiosity leads them to move toward those items. They attempt to lift their head when their neck muscles do not yet have tone. But, their curiosity pulls them to keep stretching to see what it is they heard or glimpsed. This eventually brings tone into their neck muscles, which leads to those muscles having more strength. They are able to see more.

And, then they glimpse something else, hear something else they cannot see or get to, so they stretch to see what it is. But their arm muscles have no tone. And, their curiosity keeps stretching them until they develop tone in their arm muscles. They become able to push themselves up and see more. And, on and on it goes until they are able to walk, run, skip, etc.

There is frustration that occurs when an infant cannot quite see and cannot get those muscles to work. This frustration is an indicator that there is no neural pathway developed for that activity yet. But, their curiosity keeps pulling them into mastery. These are very important skills they are developing. Learning. Working through the frustration of not yet being able. Working through making mistakes until, through their experience, they master the skill. They achieve their target.

And, now their curiosity pulls them into the next phase of development. This skill of working through a learning process is crucial to learning, growing and mastering new skills and tasks for the rest of their lives.

This is actually how neurological connections are created, how tone gets built in the muscles. The quality of tone in all muscles is an indicator of emotional and psychological health or dysfunction. As I mentioned earlier in the book, the advanced Bodynamic Practitioners can very accurately assess the emotional and psychological issues a person has just by doing a body map, assessing the tone in each muscle.

How Connection with Body Develops

When I took the Bodynamic Foundation course I learned how we connect and center with our bodies and the earth differently at different ages. In utero we connect through our umbilicus. As infants we connect through our sternum, when we are supposed to spend most of our time on our bellies. Later we connect through our sit bones when we learn to sit up. And last, we connect through our feet when we learn to stand. We are activating specific muscles and fascia during somatic connection.

The many contraptions, ie: swings, walkers, things that keep infants on their backs and off their bellies, prevent neural pathway development. These contraptions interfere with children developing the ability to connect to their own bodies and to others. I recently saw a contraption that trapped an infant in a seat, facing upward, with a video device projecting learning activities at them. Hey folks, that part of the brain is not online to do that activity yet! But parents do not have this information and they purchase these contraptions, and interfere with their child developing the neural pathways that will allow them to do that advanced learning at the appropriate time.

A person's ability to be somatically fully present is compromised by these contraptions. This affects them emotionally and psychologically, making it impossible to know what is right for them, to discharge emotion and take action based on signals they receive, to make changes in their best interest.

I have had parents say to me, "But my son (or daughter) doesn't like being on their stomach." Of course not. You allowed them to have full access to everything by keeping them on their back all of the time. Now they have lost their innate capacity to be curious about what is beyond their sight and hearing and reach for it, to reach again, to reach a bit further. To be delighted by what they discover, and have enthusiasm for what else they can reach for and accomplish. To get frustrated, struggle, and receive more from what they worked through. Do you see how the effort in itself teaches them to create in their world? To take on something they are unfamiliar with and stretch into something new? And, achieve it?

Do you notice there is an explosion of ADD and ADHD? Do you notice there is an explosion of people backing off from challenge and giving up, rather than being curious about how it could be done? Or, how else it could be done? They give up easily.

I hear parents saying, "Oh, yes, they have to have tummy time." So now they are aware it is necessary they give the child an hour a day of tummy time. No, folks, that is a limitation! Twenty-four hours a day, 7 days a week is tummy time until they move themselves to the next phase. Notice

I said *move themselves*, according to their own innate wisdom. There is an innate wisdom in each of us that organically moves us through each phase. What if we got out of the way of innate wisdom and let our children develop as they were designed to?!

Ok, now I will get off my soap box and get on with it. For more information you can check out Bette Lamont's website at: neurologicalreorganization.org, or the USA Bodynamic website at: bodynamicusa.com. Bette's work, Neurological Reorganization, has recently been recognized and supported by Bessel van der Kolk.

In some cases, people had connection skills and may have lost them after some sort of overwhelm or shock trauma, such as physical or sexual abuse, illness, chronic pain, or injury. In these cases our role is to help them rebuild their capacity.

Cultural Reinforcement for Being Disconnected

Our culture, media, pharmaceutical companies, the medical profession and our "I am too busy" lifestyles encourage the loss of somatic connection as well. There is great emphasis on medicating pain and issues without getting to the source of the problem and correcting it. For example: you have a headache. You take ibuprofen, acetaminophen or aspirin. The pain is gone. There is no encouragement to ask ourselves, "What is my headache telling me?" "How much water have I drunk today?" "Am I dehydrated?" "When was the last time I took a break?" "Am I too stressed or tense?" "Is it time to do something relaxing or self soothing?" "Am I getting ill?" Somewhere down the line people become more symptomatic;

with depression, anxiety, pain, illness, because they have not listened to themselves and taken care of themselves. They override the warning signals, disconnect. The symptoms amp up; our innate wisdom is attempting to communicate with us through the symptoms that something requires changing.

Returning to Core Stability

When someone is disconnected they report feeling in their head, scattered, confused, and often anxious and depressed. They may be able to do things cognitively, but are unable to identify what they feel physically or emotionally. They may not notice when they are hungry or tired. They may make choices based on what they "should" do rather than what is right for them. **Somatic Connection** and **Centering** activities help develop a "felt sense" of being connected and Self aware.

Being fully present and connected with your body and the earth will allow you and your client to know what is right for them. This allows you to address and resolve issues as they arise, instead of medicating or ignoring them until symptoms are severe or serious damage has occurred. If someone grew up without learning to be connected at each developmental stage, they will have to learn to connect and discover their body's own language and emotional signals. Eventually they will develop trust of their own innate Truth, their inner guidance, and core stability can emerge. The **Somatic Connection** and **Centering** activities restore your clients' connection with Self.

Chapter 17
Connection with Body, Self & Earth

How Grounding is a Limitation

I am going to take a moment here and walk you through an awareness of Truth exercise, giving you a little practice with the earlier Truth vs. Limitation activity. As you read the word "grounding," what physical and emotional signals do you get? Does it make you feel expansive, uplifted, or do you feel contracted and heavy? Most often when I ask people this question they tell me they feel heavy and contracted, and are pretty surprised at their response. When you are willing to be totally aware, you will notice how things we take for granted are actually limitations.

Let me ask you this. Which is bigger, our innate wisdom (soul, divine essence, spirit) or our body? Our innate wisdom, of course. It is infinite. Why would we teach people to stuff an infinite awareness inside a tiny body? How often do people ground their infiniteness, their soul, their spirit, into their tiny little body, so their body just keeps getting bigger to accommodate it? This was an awareness I learned in Access Consciousness® and A Course in Miracles, that put much into perspective for me about limitations that were showing up in clients who were "grounding". I have had a number of clients who have said that "grounding" always made them feel limited.

So how much awareness and Truth gets cut off when we limit our infinite capacity to be aware of everything, by grounding into our body? How much choice is lost if we cut off awareness? How easy is it for someone to get victimized because they cut off their awareness? What if clients are more vulnerable to being harmed because they have cut their awareness off by "grounding" into a small space, instead of having infinite awareness? What more could be available to choose from if we were aware of everything? What if we taught clients to have infinite awareness, so they have more choices available to them?

"But people are not in their bodies", you say. Good. What if they are being the infinite capacity they are, but have disconnected from their body and the earth due to the pain they experience? Or, they have disconnected because they are operating from the conditioning they have bought into that says a symptom is bad and wrong, so the symptom has to be shut up.

Isn't disconnection the real issue with all aspects of Self and living? Disconnection from their authentic Self, their body and the earth? What if everyone could be fully and completely present with their infinite awareness, the earth, and their body (which by the way is an amazing sensory organ)? What if they could learn to use the symptom as a pointer to what or who is not working in their life? What if people were connected with all of their awareness? Could they then make different choices and live more in alignment with their authentic Self?

Connection with Body, Self & Earth

Did you ever notice that animals are totally connected? Notice how they know when earthquakes, storms, tsunamis are coming before they show up, and they move to a safer place? Notice how some people sense things before they occur and trust their awareness and avoid disasters? While others ignore their signals and end up in the disaster, later saying they should have listened to themselves?

Several years ago I was in a 5-day class. A number of us were sitting outside eating dinner. It was warm and sunny, not a cloud in the sky. A young man, around 16 years old, suddenly looked up at the blue sky and said, "The rain is coming. We have to cover the truck with the tarp." He got up and put his plate away and headed over to the truck. His father got up to help him. Now mind you, it was still bright and sunny with absolutely no clouds in the sky. Ten minutes later storm clouds came in very quickly and it began to pour! This is an example of someone totally connected to his awareness of Self and the earth.

What if we facilitate our clients in learning to be fully and completely present? With their infiniteness, with their body and with the earth. Without limitation. Wouldn't they have more awareness, more to choose from? And, since we have already taught them to distinguish Truth from limitation, using their awareness of the subtle differences between the two, couldn't their life start working better for them?

What I will present are some somatic connection activities that allow you and your client to notice where they are connected and where they are not. This can point to missed developmental activities that we are supposed to go through while growing up, that create the neurological pathways for our connection with our bodies.

Imaginal Grounding: A Limitation

You may have heard of or done imaginal grounding exercises, but these are other than effective if a person has missed a developmental phase of somatic connection. Or if there has been some sort of overwhelm, either during a specific phase of development or from a dysregulating event. People who already have good somatic connection with their body and the earth do very well with imaginal activities, although imaginal activities are a limitation in themselves.

Why is imagination a limitation? Imagination is often a fantasy reality people make up in their heads. It is often a story they make up based on ego/personality, rather than based on their guidance from their innate wisdom. Imaginal grounding is often not a "felt sense" experience of innate wisdom's guidance. The physical and emotional reactions they are having are from what they are thinking, not from their connection to their true Self, their innate Truth.

During imaginal activities people often feel a sense of space or ease or calmness, which is misinterpreted as being grounded. But they are actually in the bliss of disconnection, which is bringing them the ease. The Truth is, when people are fully connected they perceive everything, the good, the bad and the ugly. The good news is, they are more connected. The bad news is, they are more connected. They will be aware of everything, and will require assistance in how to deal with being as aware as they really are. Once they get the "felt sense" of connection with their bodies, their awareness and choice expand dynamically.

Why do some benefit from imaginal activities and some do not? Because some people are already connected to their innate wisdom, so they are not imagining. They are aware of their innate guidance. Which gives them the core stability to be aware of everything without getting overwhelmed. When they are operating from their core stability, their innate Truth, they do not look to outside sources for what is right for them, what is true for them, for a definition of themselves. They are accessing their core stability, not their imagination.

I have worked with imaginal exercises myself over the years and found people would get a sense of more calmness in my office, but could not replicate it for themselves. In some cases they could do it on their own, but nothing was changing in their life. What I discovered is that they were in their head creating a fantasy reality. Once I added somatic activities to connect them with their innate guidance, they began to get a "felt sense" of being connected to their body and the earth, and everything changed.

"Felt Sense" Connection

Being fully and completely present and connected with your body and the earth is not for the faint of heart. Especially for people who have been traumatized. People have a fantasy that if they are more "grounded", more connected with their body and the earth, that things will get better. The good news is, they are more aware. The bad news is, they are more aware. Most people will just go back and cut off their awareness again, and go back to living in their heads. Why? Because it can be painful to be aware of everything. It can take a while to learn how to live totally aware, without taking on all of the pain. But, there is so much more choice with awareness.

Once people have reconnected to their authentic Self there is a core stability that is their foundation for everything. They do not get knocked off balance by external events any longer. Their inner guidance is always available to them. This is where their sense of security comes from. Not from what they have egoically constructed to control their world. This is another step in getting free of limitation. We move from our ego/personality trying to control and direct our lives, to being guided by our innate Truth. Then whatever comes up in life no longer is vulnerable to an unstable definition of self. You may have observed people who live Authentically being challenged by life events. They tend to observe it, consult their innate wisdom, and respond in an often matter-of-fact manner. Just another event to address in life.

Unfortunately our society is geared to being unaware, unconscious, reactive and attached to drama. We are taught to shut up the symptoms that tell us there is something going on. We are taught the symptoms are a wrongness. But they are not. Symptoms give us information. They are indicators. What makes the difference is what we do with the information, whether we judge it as right or wrong, whether we try to block it out, or use it to choose who and what works for us. When people truly become more connected to their bodies and the earth, they feel more.

Connection with Body, Self & Earth

Your job as the clinician is to help them learn to use their awareness to:

1. Identify what is True for them.
2. Identify what and who works for them.
3. Use all information they become aware of to make choices that enhance their lives.
4. Develop their trust in their innate wisdom and allow it to direct them.

For Those Who Get Overwhelmed

Clients who have extensive trauma histories, especially very early trauma, in utero trauma, torture, military mind control trauma, trauma from cult abuse, may get too overwhelmed with connecting. They have used disconnection to be able to function in the world. When they connect, they experience the pain. Their body is talking to them about what needs to be changed. These clients will require learning to control and *choose* connection and disconnection, pendulating between the two. It gives them mastery over choice instead of feeling victim to their body's communications. In this case you can have them practice connecting and disconnecting in your office, so you are there for support. You will also be using the **Containment** activities to handle strong emotions. Then have them practice at home when they feel comfortable to do so on their own.

I find the pendulating back and forth rather quickly leads them to be able to stay connected, and more willing, in time, to choose to be connected and more aware. They develop the sense they can choose, rather than having things just happen to them. They eventually discover they have more choice in their life. They are more aware of other people's motives and choices, which leads to more choice for them.

Truth vs. Limitation and Is ***This Even Mine*** activities can be used to discern what is theirs and what is not, so they stop owning what is not theirs. People also have to give up the beliefs and judgments of themselves, and others, that lock them into the pain. They have to have activities where they can get a "felt sense" of their own energy and somatic sensations to create a stable "felt sense" of self, which we have already talked about. It can be an art to facilitate clients to more ease. It takes time, patience and appropriate pacing to do so.

It is important that you use the activities earlier in this book to assess a client's ability to handle strong emotions. For you to work with the **Containment** and ***Testing Safety and Relationship*** activities prepares your clients for **Connection** and ***Centering***. When you get to this point in the resourcing, you should already be aware of what your client can handle and what they cannot. If they are easily dysregulated, be sure to spend enough time with the **Containment** activity and remind them of it before going into **Connection**. Move through the activities according to what timing and pacing works for them, so they can have a successful experience. It is crucial you are not just *doing* the activities. This is why I have put so much emphasis on developing your own awareness, and detailed communication between you and your client.

Another Awareness

I have encountered many people who say they would like to change their life, to be more present, to get out of their suffering, who, once we begin this journey to more Self awareness and Self mastery, will not choose it. They back away. They often have a fantasy reality of what "getting better" looks like. As their connection and Self awareness improve they do not like the Truth they see, or what it will actually take to get out of the limitation. Secondary gains. They wish to do the same thing they have already done and expect things around them to change. Isn't that the definition of insanity? But, I digress.

You will have to address this head-on to be able to move on. Some will choose to challenge their choices, be willing to choose what is True for them, and step out of what is creating their suffering. Some will not, or at least not now. Being more connected and Self aware does not always lead to people being willing to choose to live this way and change what causes the suffering in their lives.

Chapter 18
Connection Activities

I originally learned these **Connection** activities through the guided activities in the Bodynamic Foundation Training. There are variations I have made over the years from my own observation working with clients. The scripts are designed to use language that is as neutral as possible. My work with EMDR Therapy taught me about how much influence a word has on what people access. This awareness further expanded when I took Conscious Language Courses and became a Language of Mastery Instructor with Mastery Systems. I recommend you use them as they are written.

The **Connection** activities include a comparison of what it feels like to be connected, and what it feels like to be disconnected. Knowing what it feels like to be disconnected can be very helpful for a person to catch themselves when they disconnect. This will allow them to notice and connect again. These exercises are typically soothing, but sometimes as people connect they begin to feel things they have not been feeling, and there is some initial discomfort. Sometimes mild and sometimes more intense.

Sitting Connection Activities

As I mentioned before, we learn to connect to our bodies and the earth differently at each age. You will start with a later developmental activity, **Sitting Connection.** Why the later activity? If you go straight to the earlier-phase activities your client could have overwhelming reactions of terror if there was trauma during that phase. By starting with **Sitting Connection** you will be assessing two phases of connection.

If your client is not able to feel a connection, or a difference after connecting, there may be an earlier developmental-phase connection that has not developed. By developing the later-phase connection, your client will have more resource in their system to fall back on when it comes time to address the earlier phase. This also helps you and your client establish a teamwork relationship, so they can feel safe when it is time to do earlier resourcing. People who struggle with anxiety disorders and panic attacks could possibly be missing a very early connection resource.

The earlier-phase connections are taught in another course in the **Somatic & Energetic Resourcing** series. Having the foundational tools in this course firmly in place prepares you and your client to work with potentially dysregulating early-phase issues.

The first connection exercise is **Sitting Connection**. If your client is doing **Self Awareness—Simple** then use the **Sitting Connection—Simple** script.

Once they can move to **Self Awareness—Integrative**, switch to the **Sitting Connection—Integrative** script.

Connection Activities

If your client is already doing **Self Awareness—Integrative** then use the **Sitting Connection—Integrative** script.

- If your client is unable to feel connected with connecting through their feet while sitting, move to **Sit Bone Connection**.
- If your client can feel the connection through their sit bones, then return to connection through their feet while sitting and see if they now can feel connected through their feet.
- If they cannot get the "felt sense" of the connection, have them practice both until they develop the connection.

This will be more clear when you read the script.

If your client cannot get more connection, or prefers to be in the disconnected state when you do the activity with them, have them practice the connection activity for a week or two to see if this improves. If it does not, there may be an early developmental connection problem (addressed in a different course), or there could be some neurological deficits which should be assessed.

Have your client only practice the connection. The disconnection in the script is just for them to notice the difference. We prefer they practice being connected.

Warning

If at any time your client becomes overwhelmed when connecting, simply have them lift their toes to disconnect, have them do **Containment** and then do something self soothing, and practice this exercise **only with you** until they can safely do so on their own.

Prescription

- Continue **Self Awareness** 4 times a day.
- Do **Sitting Connection** at least once a day. They can do this more often per day if they wish, or as is useful.

Have them write down the date and time of day they practiced, and bring this information in next session. If they are having trouble complying, make sure to practice in your office each session. There are CDs and MP3 downloads available through my retail website: transformativeproductions.com. I recorded them for those clients who are having difficulty doing this on their own.

Sitting Connection—Simple (Script)

I invite you to close your eyes,

Turning your awareness to the bottoms of your feet.

Notice how your feet connect to the floor.

Notice if the contact between your feet and the floor is evenly distributed,

Or, if there is more contact on the outside bottoms of your feet,

inside bottoms of your feet,

back on your heel,

or up on the ball of your foot.

Notice if there is a difference between how your right and your left foot connect to the floor.

> *(Have your client give you feedback about what they are experiencing so far, then return their awareness to the bottoms of their feet.)*

Now very gently hold the floor with your toes. *(Wait 2–3 seconds)*

And let them go.

Again, very gently grip the floor with your toes. *(Wait 2–3 seconds)*

And let them go.

What do you notice now?

> *(Have them describe to you what they experience. Specifically, you are looking for changes in how the bottoms of their feet connect to the floor. Is the contact more evenly distributed? Is the contact close to the same on both feet? They may describe other things,*

> *ie: more energy in their feet or legs, or their feet feel heavier, which indicates more connection. And it is important that contact becomes more even.)*

Return your attention to the bottoms of your feet. *(Give them a couple of seconds to connect.)*

And for comparison,

This time lift your toes off the floor. *(Wait 2–3 seconds.)*

And lay them down. *(Wait 2–3 seconds.)*

And again lift your toes off the floor. *(Wait 2–3 seconds.)*

And lay them down. *(Wait 2–3 seconds.)*

What do you notice now? *(Give them time to describe.)*

> *(They should describe less contact, or less even contact. Sometimes people will report more contact, which should indicate the next toe grip will improve their connection more. This is a disconnection activity so they can compare the difference between being connected and being disconnected.)*

Return your awareness to the bottoms of your feet. *(Give them a couple of seconds to connect.)*

Slightly hold the floor with your toes. *(Wait 2–3 seconds.)*

And let them go.

And again slightly hold the floor with your toes. *(Wait 2–3 seconds.)*

And let them go.

What do you notice now? *(Give them time to describe.)*

Connection Activities

(They should notice more even connection with the floor and more contact, ie: their feet feel heavier or more connected with the floor.)

Note: If they report no change in connection, then have them do sit bone connection and then return to connection through their feet.

Somatic & Energetic Resourcing

Sit Bone Connection

Turn your awareness to your sit bones.

Notice how your sit bones connect to the cushion beneath you.

Notice if the contact is even, or if one side is more connected than the other.

Now press your sit bones into the cushion beneath you.

Making contact right to left.

And forward and backward.

And now what do you notice? *(Give them time to describe.)*

> *(Their sit bones should be more evenly contacting the cushion. If not, have them do it again until they get more contact. Then return to connection through their feet.)*

Return your awareness to the bottoms of your feet. *(Give them a couple of seconds to connect.)*

Slightly hold the floor with your toes. *(Wait 2–3 seconds.)*

And let them go.

And again slightly hold the floor with your toes. *(Wait 2–3 seconds.)*

And let them go.

What do you notice now? *(Give them time to describe.)*

> *(They should notice more even connection with the floor and more contact. If they do not, have them practice sit bone connection and sitting connection and see if they develop more contact.)*

Connection Activities

Note: If your client consistently practices connection and does not develop connection, there may be an even earlier connection problem, or they may have some neurological deficits that should be assessed.

Somatic & Energetic Resourcing

Debra A. Littrell
Transformative Spirit, LLC

Somatic & Energetic Resourcing™

Self Awareness & Sitting Connection Homework—Simple

1. Do the *Self Awareness* exercise four times a day. Fill in the date, day of the week, and the times of day you completed each *Self Awareness* practice session and note what sensations, emotions and thought qualities you experienced during the activity.

2. Fill in the time of day you completed your *Sitting Connection* exercise. *Sitting Connection* is only required once a day and you can combine it with one of your *Self Awareness* practices. HOWEVER, IF YOU LIKE, you can do *Sitting Connection* more than once a day.

Bring this sheet back with you to your next session.

Self Awareness	Date:	Day of the Week:
Time	Sensations, Emotions & Thought Qualities you experienced	
Sitting Connection	Time	

Self Awareness	Date:	Day of the Week:
Time	Sensations, Emotions & Thought Qualities you experienced	
Sitting Connection	Time	

© Copyright 2013 Debra Littrell All Rights Reserved. You may make copies to use in your own practice with your clients only. Otherwise this material cannot be altered, copied, or translated without the express, written permission of Debra A. Littrell.

Figure 5: Sitting Connection—Simple
Page 1 of 3

Sitting Connection—Integrative (Script)

I invite you to close your eyes,

Scanning your body.

Notice what sensations are present. *(Wait 2–3 seconds)*

Notice what emotions are present. *(Wait 2–3 seconds)*

Notice the quality of your thoughts. *(Wait 2–3 seconds)*

Turning your awareness to the bottoms of your feet.

Notice how your feet connect to the floor.

Notice if the contact between your feet and the floor is evenly distributed,

or if there is more contact on the outside bottoms of your feet,

inside bottoms of your feet,

back on the heel,

or up on the ball of your foot.

Notice if there is a difference between how your right and your left foot connect to the floor.

> *(Have your client describe what they are experiencing, in their body, emotions and thought quality so far, then return their awareness to the bottoms of their feet.)*

Now very gently hold the floor with your toes. *(Wait 2–3 seconds)*

And let them go.

Again very gently hold the floor with your toes. *(Wait 2–3 seconds)*

Somatic & Energetic Resourcing

And let them go.

What do you notice now about how your feet connect to the floor? *(Wait 2–3 seconds)*

And with more connection is there any difference in your body? *(Wait 2–3 seconds)*

In your emotions?

> *(Have them describe to you what they experience. Specifically you are looking for changes in how the bottoms of their feet connect to the floor. Is the contact more evenly distributed? Is the contact closer to the same on both feet? Is there any difference in their body, emotions or thought quality with more connection? They may describe other things ie: more energy in their feet or legs, or their feet feel heavier, which indicates more connection . And, it is important that contact becomes more even.)*

Return your attention to the bottoms of your feet. *(Give them a couple of seconds to connect.)*

And for comparison,

This time lift your toes off the floor. *(Wait 2–3 seconds.)*

And lay them down. *(Wait 2–3 seconds.)*

And again lift your toes off the floor. *(Wait 2–3 seconds.)*

And lay them down. *(Wait 2–3 seconds.)*

What do you notice now about how your feet connect to the floor? *(Wait 2–3 seconds)*

Connection Activities

And is there any difference in your body? *(Wait 2–3 seconds)*

In your emotions? *(Give them time to describe.)*

> *(What is different in the bottoms of their feet, body, emotions, and thought quality? They should describe less contact, or less even contact.*
>
> *Here they are learning how their body, emotions and thought quality will signal them if they lose their connection, so they can be aware and connect themselves.*
>
> *Sometimes people will report more contact, which should indicate the next toe grip will improve their connection more. This is a disconnection activity so they can compare the difference between being connected and being disconnected.)*

Return your awareness to the bottoms of your feet. *(Give them a couple of seconds to connect.)*

Slightly hold the floor with your toes. *(Wait 2–3 seconds.)*

And let them go.

And again slightly hold the floor with your toes. *(Wait 2–3 seconds.)*

And let them go.

What do you notice now about how your feet connect to the floor? *(Wait 2–3 seconds)*

And is there any difference in your body? *(Wait 2–3 seconds)*

In your emotions? *(Give them time to describe.)*

> *(They should notice more even connection with the floor and more contact, ie: their feet feel heavier or*

Somatic & Energetic Resourcing

more planted, connected with the floor. They should become more aware of how their body, emotions and thought quality signal them that they are connected.)

Note: If they report no change in connection, then have them do sit bone connection and then return to connecting through their feet.

Connection Activities

Sit Bone Connection

Turn your awareness to your sit bones.

Notice how your sit bones connect to the cushion beneath you.

Notice if the contact is even, or if one side is more connected than the other.

Now press your sit bones into the cushion beneath you.

Making contact right to left.

And forward and backward.

And now what do you notice now about how your sit bones connect to the cushion beneath you?

What do you notice in your body? *(Wait 2–3 seconds)*

In your emotions? *(Give them time to describe.)*

> *(Their sit bones should be more evenly contacting the cushion. If not, have them do it again until they get more contact. Then return to connection through their feet.)*

Return your awareness to the bottoms of your feet. *(Give them a couple of seconds to connect.)*

Slightly hold the floor with your toes. *(Wait 2–3 seconds.)*

And let them go.

And again slightly hold the floor with your toes. *(Wait 2–3 seconds.)*

And let them go.

Somatic & Energetic Resourcing

What do you notice now about how your feet connect to the floor? *(Wait 2–3 seconds)*

What is different in your body? *(Wait 2–3 seconds)*

In your emotions? *(Give them time to describe.)*
> *(They should notice more even connection with the floor, and what their body sensations, emotions and thought qualities are like when connected. If they do not, have them practice sit bone connection and sitting connection, and see if they develop more contact.)*

Note: If your client consistently practices connection and does not develop connection, there may be an even earlier connection problem, or they may have some neurological deficits that should be assessed. Injuries they may have had during their life may also cut their connection. Sometimes the connection activity will repair the disconnection.

Connection Activities

Somatic & Energetic Resourcing™

Self Awareness & Sitting Connection Homework—Integrative

1. Do the *Self Awareness* exercise four times a day Fill in the date, day of the week and then note the time of day you completed each *Self Awareness* practice session.

2. Fill in the time of day you completed your *Sitting Connection* exercise. You can combine one *Self Awareness* exercise with your *Sitting Connection* exercise. IF YOU LIKE, you can do *Sitting Connection* more than once a day.

Bring this sheet back with you to your next session.

Date:								
Day of Week:								
Morning Time:								
Lunch Time:								
Dinner Time:								
Bedtime:								
Sitting Connection								

© Copyright 2013 Debra Littrell All Rights Reserved. You may make copies to use in your own practice with your clients only. Otherwise this material cannot be altered, copied, or translated without the express, written permission of Debra A. Littrell.

Figure 6: Sitting Connection—Integrative
Page 1 of 2

Standing Connection Activities

Standing Connection can be added the following week unless your client is having difficulty with ***Sitting Connection***. If you need to, do ***Sitting Connection*** with them in the office to reinforce their homework until they can connect easily. Then move to ***Standing Connection***.

Standing Connection gives your client more ability to stay connected with Self when moving about in the world. It is a stepping stone in developing the sense of confidence and knowing what is correct for them. There is also a sense of ease in moving through the world.

If your client is doing ***Self Awareness—Simple*** then use the ***Standing Connection—Simple*** script.

Once they can move to ***Self Awareness—Integrative***, switch to the ***Standing Connection—Integrative*** script.

If your client is already doing ***Self Awareness—Integrative*** then use the ***Standing Connection—Integrative*** script.

Prescription

- Continue *Self Awareness* 4 times a day.
- Add *Sitting Connection* at least once a day. They can do this more often per day if they wish, or as is useful.
- Do *Standing Connection* at least once a day. They can do this more often in a day if they wish, or as is useful.

Have them write down the date and time of day they practiced, and bring this information in next session. If they are having trouble complying, make sure to practice in your office each session. There are CDs and MP3 downloads available through my retail website: transformativeproductions.com. I recorded them for those clients who are having difficulty doing this on their own.

Somatic & Energetic Resourcing

Standing Connection (Script)

Standing Up

Centering your weight evenly between your feet.

I invite you to scan your body from head to toe.

Notice what sensations are present and how you stand. *(Wait 2–3 seconds)*

Notice what emotions you are experiencing. *(Wait 2–3 seconds)*

And notice the quality of your thoughts. *(Wait 2–3 seconds)*

You don't have to do anything about them.

Just notice what you are experiencing.

Turning your awareness to the bottoms of your feet,

Notice how they connect to the floor.

Notice if your connection is evenly distributed around the bottoms of your feet. *(Wait 2–3 seconds)*

Or if there is more contact on the outside bottoms, *(Wait 2–3 seconds)*

The inside bottoms, *(Wait 2–3 seconds)*

Back on your heel, *(Wait 2–3 seconds)*

Or up on the balls or your feet. *(Wait 2–3 seconds)*

Notice if there is a difference between your right and left foot. *(Wait 2–3 seconds)*

(Have them describe to you what they notice.)

Now walking slowly,

Connection Activities

Notice how you walk through your feet. *(Wait 2–3 seconds)*

Noticing if you walk more on the outside bottoms of your feet, *(Wait 2–3 seconds)*

The inside bottoms of your feet, *(Wait 2–3 seconds)*

Or through the center of your feet. *(Wait 2–3 seconds)*

Noticing what your balance is like. *(Wait 2–3 seconds)*

Noticing your posture. *(Wait 2–3 seconds)*

How you hold your shoulders. *(Wait 2–3 seconds)*

And how you are holding your head. *(Wait 2–3 seconds)*

Noticing how the right and left sides of your body work together.

And how the top and bottom halves of your body work together as you walk.

Now stopping. *(Have them describe to you what they notice.)*

We are going to connect one foot.

Choose which foot you would like to start with.

Gently pressing the heel of your foot into the floor, *(Wait 2–3 seconds)*

Feeling the contact, the connection. *(Wait 2–3 seconds)*

Rolling it around a little, feeling the connection between your foot and the floor. *(Wait 2–3 seconds)*

Focus on the "felt sense" of that connection. *(Wait 2–3 seconds)*

Now pressing the outside bottom of your foot into the floor,

Rolling it back and forth, *(Wait 2–3 seconds)*

Feeling contact, *(Wait 2–3 seconds)*

Somatic & Energetic Resourcing

Noticing the sensations of the connection of your foot with the floor. *(Wait 2–3 seconds)*

And gently pressing the inside bottom of your foot into the floor, **being careful of your knee.** *(Wait 2–3 seconds)*

Rolling it back and forth, *(Wait 2–3 seconds)*

Feeling the contact between the floor and the inside bottom of your foot. *(Wait 2–3 seconds)*

Noticing the sensations of your connection. *(Wait 2–3 seconds)*

And pressing the ball of your foot into the floor. *(Wait 2–3 seconds)*

Rolling it around. *(Wait 2–3 seconds)*

Feeling the contact. *(Wait 2–3 seconds)*

Feeling the connection. *(Wait 2–3 seconds)*

Now standing up evenly on both feet,

Check the bottoms of your feet.

Notice what is different now that you have connected one foot. *(Wait 2–3 seconds)*

Notice what the contact is like now between your feet and the floor. *(Wait 2–3 seconds)*

Noticing what's different. *(Have them describe to you what is different.)*

Noticing if there is any difference between the right and left sides of your body.

(Have them describe to you what is different.)

Now walking.

Connection Activities

Notice how you are walking through your feet. *(Wait 2–3 seconds)*

What the difference is now between the right and the left. *(Wait 2–3 seconds)*

Noticing your balance. *(Wait 2–3 seconds)*

Noticing your posture. *(Wait 2–3 seconds)*

Your shoulders and your head. *(Wait 2–3 seconds)*

(Have them describe to you what is different.)

Now we will connect the other foot.

Gently pressing the heel of your foot into the floor. *(Wait 2–3 seconds)*

Feeling the contact, the connection. *(Wait 2–3 seconds)*

Rolling it around a little, feeling the connection between your foot and the floor. *(Wait 2–3 seconds)*

Focus on the "felt sense" of that connection. *(Wait 2–3 seconds)*

Now pressing the outside bottom of your foot into the floor.

Rolling it back and forth. *(Wait 2–3 seconds)*

Feeling contact. *(Wait 2–3 seconds)*

Noticing the sensations of the connection of your foot with the floor. *(Wait 2–3 seconds)*

And gently pressing the inside bottom of your foot into the floor, being careful of your knee. *(Wait 2–3 seconds)*

Rolling it back and forth. *(Wait 2–3 seconds)*

Feeling the contact between the floor and the inside bottom of your foot. *(Wait 2–3 seconds)*

Somatic & Energetic Resourcing

Noticing the sensations of your connection. *(Wait 2–3 seconds)*

And pressing the ball of your foot into the floor. *(Wait 2–3 seconds)*

Rolling it around. *(Wait 2–3 seconds)*

Feeling the contact. *(Wait 2–3 seconds)*

Feeling the connection. *(Wait 2–3 seconds)*

Now standing evenly on both feet,

Checking the bottoms of your feet,

And notice what is different in how your feet connect to the floor. *(Wait 2–3 seconds)*

Scan your body and notice what is different. *(Wait 2–3 seconds)*

> *(Have them describe to you what is different.)*

Now walking.

Notice how you are walking through your feet, *(Wait 2–3 seconds)*

What the difference is now between the right and the left, *(Wait 2–3 seconds)*

Noticing your balance. *(Wait 2–3 seconds)*

Noticing your posture. *(Wait 2–3 seconds)*

Your shoulders and your head. *(Wait 2–3 seconds)*

> *(Have them describe to you what is different.)*

Now stopping.

Connection Activities

If your client is still uneven in how their feet connect to the floor have them:

Connect both heels at the same time. *(Wait 2–3 seconds)*

Connect the outside bottoms at the same time. *(Wait 2–3 seconds)*

Connect the inside bottoms at the same time, being careful of your knee. *(Wait 2–3 seconds)*

Connect the balls of your feet at the same time. *(Wait 2–3 seconds)*

Stand still.

Check the bottoms of your feet. *(Wait 2–3 seconds)*

And notice how they connect to the floor. *(Wait 2–3 seconds)*

Scan your body from head to toe,

And notice what's different. *(Wait 2–3 seconds)*

Checking in with your emotions and noticing what you are experiencing now. *(Wait 2–3 seconds)*

And noticing the quality of your thinking. *(Wait 2–3 seconds)*

(Have them describe to you what is different.)

Note: They should notice more even connection with the floor, and what their body sensations, emotions and thought qualities are like when connected. When people are more connected they often report feeling their feet feel heavier, the contact more evenly distributed around the bottoms of their feet, or feeling as if their feet are being pulled into the earth like a magnet. They often report feeling more upright when they stand and walk. They stand straighter, feel more confident, their mood lightens. They often have better balance and feel coordinated when they walk. People often report feeling like they are gliding when they walk. These are just a few of the comments you may hear.

Connection Activities

Somatic & Energetic Resourcing™

Self Awareness, Sitting & Standing Connection Homework—Simple

1. Do the ***Self Awareness*** exercise four times a day. Fill in the date, day of the week & time of day you completed each ***Self Awareness*** practice session. Note what sensations, emotions and thought qualities you experienced during the activity.

2. Fill in the time of day you completed your ***Sitting & Standing Connection*** exercises. ***Sitting & Standing Connection*** are only required once a day. HOWEVER, IF YOU LIKE, you can do ***Sitting & Standing Connection*** more than once a day.

Bring this sheet back with you to your next session.

Self Awareness	Date: Day of the Week:		Day of the Week:	
Time	Sensations, Emotions & Thought Qualities you experienced			
Sitting Connection	Time:		**Standing Connection**	Time:

Self Awareness	Date:		Day of the Week:	
Time	Sensations, Emotions & Thought Qualities you experienced			
Sitting Connection	Time:		**Standing Connection**	Time:

© Copyright 2013 Debra Littrell All Rights Reserved. You may make copies to use in your own practice with your clients only. Otherwise this material cannot be altered, copied, or translated without the express, written permission of Debra A. Littrell.

Figure 7: Standing Connection—Simple
Page 1 of 3

Somatic & Energetic Resourcing

Somatic & Energetic Resourcing™

Self Awareness, Sitting & Standing Connection
Homework—Integrative

1. Do the *Self Awareness* activity four times a day. Fill in the date, day of the week and then note the time of day you completed each *Self Awareness* practice session.

2. Fill in the time of day you completed your *Sitting & Standing Connection* activities. *Sitting & Standing Connection* activities are only required once a day. IF YOU LIKE, you can do them more than once a day.

Bring this sheet back with you to your next session.

Date:							
Day of Week:							
Morning Time:							
Lunch Time:							
Dinner Time:							
Bedtime:							
Sitting Connection:							
Standing Connection:							

© Copyright 2013 Debra Littrell All Rights Reserved. You may make copies to use in your own practice with your clients only. Otherwise this material cannot be altered, copied, or translated without the express, written permission of Debra A. Littrell.

Figure 8: Standing Connection—Integrative
Page 1 of 2

What Am I Assessing When I Do These Activities with My Clients?

When I do **Self Awareness** and **Connection** Activities they tell me:

- Can my client name a sensation? (primitive brain function, possible dissociation)
- Can they name emotions? (primitive brain function, possible dissociation)
- Are they giving me clear, accurate feedback?
- Are they trying to look for what I want?
- Are they able to stay connected with Self while in conversation with me? (dual focus)
- If they do not have the resource, does it begin to develop as they repeat the activities?
- Do these resources begin to spontaneously show up in their daily lives?
- Do they get overwhelmed when they are connected with Self?
- Do they begin to report that they are becoming Self aware more often in their daily life?
- Do they develop the capacity to be Self aware most of the time during their daily life?
- What shows up differently in the choices they make when they are more Self aware and connected in their daily life?

Chapter 19
Centering

Centering activities assist clients in further knowing what is right for them and taking action accordingly. Typically, if a person is other than aware of their center you will find their core muscles are either too rigid or have no tone. Activities such as pilates and yoga are very good for building core muscles if the instructor is good at assisting people in locating and activating their core muscles consciously. Some classes are taught by instructors who have their own Self awareness deficits, or the classes are more about looking good and being in competition. Finding good instructors to refer to can be very helpful to your clients.

Exercise balls work very well for bringing tone into core muscles. Having them available in your office is useful for you to guide your clients in how to use them. Exercise balls come in various sizes so clients must buy one according to their height and pump it up, so when they sit on it their thighs and lower legs form a 90° angle.

Somatic & Energetic Resourcing

Centering Prescription 1

If your client finds it challenging to sit on the ball for very long, have them work up, starting with one minute and adding one minute each day. Once they have built more tone, encourage them to watch TV on it, work on their computer on it, talk on the phone on it, etc. Assigning clients to use a ball to sit on at work, instead of a chair, is an excellent way to strengthen their core muscles. I assign clients who are in the computer industry to do so since posture is often an issue with long hours on a computer. The ball helps them stay in a neutral position, strengthens their core muscles and increases productivity. They may have to work their way up to being able to use it all day. Just have them start with what is comfortable and gradually increase their time on the ball each day.

Building tone in core muscles gives us a sense of knowing what is right for us, confidence, clarity and assertiveness.

Psoas

Our psoas muscle, located deep in our pelvis, is also responsible for giving us a sense of knowing what is right for us, confidence, a sense of clarity, and ease in asserting ourselves. Sometimes a client's psoas is either too rigid or lacks tone. This can show up as either controlling behavior or difficulty in knowing what is right for them and speaking up.

Warning: This activity is best learned in person in a class, in case consultation or in your own individual session. If you have any questions about the script that is provided, or if your client reports discomfort, stop the activity and seek consultation.

Centering Prescription 2

1. Have your client do **Standing Connection** first and then **Psoas Centering**.
2. When resourcing the psoas, lifting and turning movements are very slow and deliberate.
3. Make sure they are lifting with their psoas, not their thigh.
4. Start with one lift, turn. If it is easy, try two. When they get to the place where it is a challenge, have them start with that number until it gets easy, then add one.
5. **The most number of repetitions that will ever be done is 5.** (More can throw your client's life into chaos.)
6. **Psoas Centering is only to be done once a day.** (More can throw your client's life into chaos.)

Somatic & Energetic Resourcing

Psoas Centering (Script)

Use the *Standing Connection* script first so your client is fully connected, then continue on with *Psoas Centering*.

Lie down on the floor.

Point your toes to the ceiling with your feet gently flexed.

Place your fingers on the upper edges of your hip bones, then slide the fingers of each hand about an inch along an imaginary V toward your pubic bone.

Attempt to lift your leg and feel the muscle under your fingers.

This is the psoas muscle. *(If your client has difficulty finding the psoas, this is where they have to start, learning to lift with their psoas, not their thigh muscle.)*

> *(Assign only one lift and turn until they can clearly isolate and use their psoas muscle.)*

Press your Left heel into the ground to take the pressure off of your lower back.

Allow your Right foot to rotate slightly out with your foot still gently flexed.

Concentrate on lifting your Right leg using your psoas muscle under your fingers. Avoid using your thigh muscle.

Lift your Right leg slowly so your heel is even with your Left toes.

Slowly lower your leg back to the ground.

Now rotate your Right foot back to where your toes are pointing to the ceiling again.

Centering

(If this was easy for your client, have them add one more lift. If this was difficult, then they will only be doing one lift to start with. If they are having difficulty with isolating and using their psoas muscle they will start with one lift, practicing finding and using their muscle.)

Now press your Right heel into the floor to protect your lower back.

Rotate your Left foot out, keeping your foot <u>gently</u> flexed.

Concentrate on lifting your Left leg using your psoas muscle under your fingers. Avoid using your thigh muscle.

(Have your client lift their Left leg the same number of times as they lifted their Right.)

Lift your Left leg slowly until your heel is even with your Right toes.

Slowly lower your leg back to the ground.

Now rotate your Left foot back to where your toes are pointing <u>gently</u> to the ceiling again.

Now press your Left heel into the floor to protect your lower back.

Slowly lift your Right leg using your psoas, until your heel is even with your Left toes.

Slowly rotate your Right leg out, then in, keeping your toes <u>gently</u> flexed.

(Have your client rotate the same number of times as they lifted before.)

Somatic & Energetic Resourcing

Rotate your Right leg back to center with your toes <u>gently</u> pointed to the ceiling.

Slowly lower your Right leg.

Now press your Right heel into the floor to protect your lower back.

Slowly lift your Left leg using your psoas, until your heel is even with your Right toes.

Slowly rotate your Left leg out, then in, keeping your toes <u>gently</u> flexed.

> *(Have your client rotate the same number of times as they lifted before.)*

Rotate your Left leg back to center with your toes <u>gently</u> pointed to the ceiling.

Slowly lower your Left leg.

When doing this exercise you must focus on your psoas muscle to make sure you are using it.

Movements must be slow and controlled.

Once one lift and turn is easy, add a second. When two is easy, add a third. When three is easy, add a fourth. When four is easy, add a fifth. ***Five is the most you will ever do.*** This activity is designed to bring awareness and tone into your psoas. We are not building muscle. ***Too many, too fast can throw your life into chaos.***

Only do this activity once a day. If you do this more than once a day you will throw your life into chaos.

Doing psoas centering as prescribed can bring a sense of confidence and knowing what is right for you.

Somatic & Energetic Resourcing

Debra A. Littrell
Transformative Spirit, LLC

Somatic & Energetic Resourcing™

Self Awareness, Sitting & Standing Connection & Centering Homework—Simple

1. Do the ***Self Awareness*** activity four times a day. Fill in the date, day of the week, and time of day you completed each ***Self Awareness*** practice. Note what sensations, emotions and thought qualities you experienced during the activity.

2. Fill in the time of day you completed your ***Sitting Connection, Standing Connection & Centering*** activities. ***Sitting & Standing Connection*** are **only required once a day**. HOWEVER, IF YOU LIKE, you can do them more than once. **_Only do Centering once a day._**

Bring this sheet back with you to your next session.

Self Awareness	Date:		Day of the Week:	
Time	Sensations, Emotions & Thought Qualities you experienced			
Sitting Connection	Time:	Standing Connection & Centering		Time:

Self Awareness	Date:		Day of the Week:	
Time	Sensations, Emotions & Thought Qualities you experienced			
Sitting Connection	Time:	Standing Connection & Centering		Time:

© Copyright 2013 Debra Littrell. All Rights Reserved. You may make copies to use in your own practice with your clients only. Otherwise this material cannot be altered, copied, or translated without the express, written permission of Debra A. Littrell.

Figure 9: Centering—Simple
Page 1 of 3

Centering

Debra A. Littrell
Transformative Spirit, LLC

Somatic & Energetic Resourcing™

***Self Awareness, Sitting & Standing Connection,
Centering—Integrative Homework***

1. Do the ***Self Awareness*** activity four times a day. Fill in the date, day of the week and then note the time of day you completed each ***Self Awareness*** practice session.
2. Fill in the time of day you completed your ***Sitting Connection, Standing Connection & Centering*** activities.
Sitting & Standing Connection are **only required once a day**. HOWEVER, IF YOU LIKE, you can do ***Sitting & Standing Connection*** more than once a day.

Only do centering once a day.

Bring this sheet back with you to your next session.

Self Awareness: Practice four times a day.							
Date:							
Day of Week:							
Morning Time:							
Lunch Time:							
Dinner Time:							
Bedtime:							

	Time of Day: Practice each connection activity at least once a day (more is ok). **ONLY PRACTICE CENTERING ONCE A DAY!!!!!!!!!!!!!**						
Sitting Connection							
Standing Connection & Centering							

© Copyright 2013 Debra Littrell All Rights Reserved. You may make copies to use in your own practice with your clients only. Otherwise this material cannot be altered, copied, or translated without the express, written permission of Debra A. Littrell.

*Figure 10: Centering—Integrative
Page 1 of 2*

What Am I Assessing When I Do This Activity with My Clients?

The *Centering* activities help me assess:

- Do they have a sense of knowing what is right for them?
- Does their ability to know what is correct for them develop? And does it stay with them in their daily lives?
- Do they get a sense of confidence?
- Does that strengthen and generalize to their lives?

Chapter 20
In Conclusion

Thank you for taking the time to read this book, develop the resources in yourself and contributing them to your clients. Please remember, if you don't have them you cannot transmit them. If you find they "don't work" there are a number of questions to ask.

1. Do I have the resource myself?
2. Am I looking for a result?
3. If it "doesn't work," is the activity showing me where the client's resource is missing?
4. If the repeated use of the resource is not building the resource in, is there an underlying neurological issue that requires attention?
5. Is the client not willing to go there? Is there some secondary gain for not changing that needs to be addressed first?

Also, a reminder, that rereading this book a few times can help you clear whatever limitations come up, and allow you to gain a deeper awareness of how to do the activities and how they work. As I mentioned earlier, both of my editors found their awareness of, and capacity to work with, this information went much deeper with repeated readings. If you ran into

Somatic & Energetic Resourcing

a number of places you were not clear about the information, be sure to go back over them a few times.

I find they always "work". The activities tell me a great deal about my client. What resources they have, what they don't, if there are serious developmental issues that need to be repaired, if there is a neurological underpinning that needs to be addressed, if there is a blocking belief, if they just don't want to. This is why I said in the beginning, the activities are diagnostic. I don't look for results. I use them to identify what is going on. You will see a wide spectrum of responses. It is all useful information. Then my question is, how do we change any limitations that are showing up?

One of the things I find myself explaining to my clients is, this work will not make sense. In this work, one plus one may equal three thousand. When the resources are taking hold your client will simply find themselves responding differently, organically, with ease. They may be surprised how easily they handle previously anxiety-provoking situations. Why? Their body quits signalling them, through symptoms, that it requires something. When it gets what it requires the symptoms stop and your client just handles things. Your left brain and your client's will not be able to figure it out or predict what can occur. I encourage my clients to do an experiment. To suspend their attempt to figure it out and see what shows up. They often are surprised at how experiencing the activities makes changes without efforting. And, they are relieved. In so many ways.

There are many clients who will "pick up the ball and run" with these activities. You will see things dramatically change in their lives in a very short period of time. Organically. With-

In Conclusion

out effort, other than just experiencing the activities. And, now they have the resources to use throughout their lives, and can revisit the activities any time they would like.

There are other clients who will complain about how much effort it takes to practice the activities or pay attention to themselves. Then this is where the work is. It can be tedious to have to do the activities in your office each session until they can take them over. But it can pay off. It will be the difference between living unaware, disconnected from innate Truth, unable to regulate their emotions, unable to take in support; and having everything change.

I have a friend and colleague who works with clients who are highly dissociative, victims of military mind control experiments, victims of satanic cult abuse, etc. She uses these activities with them. It is tedious work and it may take years before they are able to really take in the resource, but she gets results. Her measuring stick for change is very different than the quick-fix expectations the profession has been moving to. She even reports that her clients function much better than most people when they allow themselves to receive the resources, both the energetic and somatic resources. She is finding the energetic resourcing is even more powerful for building the platform for the rest of their work. Why? Dissociative people are already very energetically aware. No one has taught them how to use it for themselves. They learn how to use their energetic awareness as a resource. She starts with the energetic resources, then moves to the somatic resources, and then is able to do the trauma resolution work.

It is always nice when you have a mix of people in your practice, those who can really receive from the activities and those who will take time to develop the resources. I find that just taking some time at the beginning of each session to do the activities, and then move on to use other tools for clearing limitation during the rest of the session, provides the consistency these folks require. In time, they begin to open up and receive. And, you get the regular practice right along with them.

A few of these activities are used in a variety of body-centered psychotherapies. Many of them share the same activities. I have taken, and adapted them to use for assessment and preparation work. Others I created myself. If you find yourself looking for really detailed training in body-centered, developmental work, I highly recommend the Bodynamic Training, which originated in Denmark. You will find the websites for the Bodynamic International and the Bodynamic USA Training Institutes in the Resources and Recommended Readings section. What is great about taking these more in-depth courses is that it interrupts your old style on a routine basis, allowing a gradual change to a more authentic way of practicing. Just be ready to learn to practice in a completely different way than the current industry standard. More Authentically!

I will be making the Practitioner's Checklist and the Homework forms available for sale in a store I am building on my retail site, transformativeproductions.com. You will receive it at a discount by entering the coupon code SERBook as a thank you for purchasing this book. If the store is not up and running when you arrive, use the contact form to request your copy and I will make arrangements to get it to you.

In Conclusion

The resources I have shared in this book are just the beginning. There is more on awareness and sorting out what is theirs and what they have taken on from others in the next course. I cover "boundary" work in the second course, but I will be renaming that as well. I have found that most "boundary" work is people learning to put up walls, which cuts off awareness and makes people more vulnerable.

The work I do around "boundaries", personal space, energetic awareness of one's Self and others is powerful. Clients really get benefit from the activities, but they have to have enough Self awareness and ability to communicate with me during the activity. Their relationship with me has to be safe and open. They have to be able to contain emotions that may come up. They have to have all of the skills we have covered in this course first, for "boundary" work to be done safely and effectively. It is very delicate work and requires studying the details of what shows up throughout the various phases of the activities. I have seen many people change dramatically and spontaneously from these activities.

If you would like help with building these resources for yourself, or in learning how to work with your clients with these tools, I am available for consultation. Some of the activities are difficult to describe in writing, and pictures do not always show the details. If you are unsure, or have any difficulty, contact me. I often do consultation via video conferencing, allowing me to see how you are doing activities and to be able to demonstrate activities.

Clients should never experience harmful pain when doing these activities. They may get connected enough to have physical or emotional pain from what has been stored in their

Somatic & Energetic Resourcing

system for so long. This is not harm. This is awareness. This is why I have given you some tools for containment and regulation. This is different than pain that causes harm. If they have injuries of any kind, consult with their physician or physical therapist about what the client can and cannot do.

I have seen these activities repair physical issues as well. I had one physical therapist come in and learn some of the activities because the centering activities I did with a mutual client changed some physical issues they had been trying to resolve.

Please work safely with these activities, and get consultation if you have any questions. For people who have been severely traumatized, you will have to go slow and pendulate the activities as described, so they learn they can have choice over what occurs. A powerful resource, choice.

You may have to "work the edges" with some clients. There is much conditioning about disconnecting and not feeling, and that there is something "wrong" if they feel physical or emotional pain. Then they get into the blame game. They may have to be re-educated about how the signals are a pointer to what is asking to change. You may have to work with them to study the subtle difference between what is not true for them, and what is their body trying to release what has been locked up in it for a long time.

Have fun. Enjoy the journey. And, let me know if you could use some assistance in implementing the activities.

Resources & Recommended Readings

Bartlett, R., (2009). *The Physics of Miracles* (Ch. 9, pp. 67–68). New York, NY: Simon & Schuster, Inc.

Korn, D., & Leeds, A. (2002, December). Preliminary Evidence of Efficacy for EMDR Resource Development and Installation in the Stabilization Phase of Treatment of Complex Posttraumatic Stress Disorder. *Journal of Clinical Psychology*, 58(12), pp. 1465–1487. doi:10.1002/jclp.10099.

Kurtz, R. (1990). *Body Centered Psychotherapy: The Hakomi Method.* Mendocino, CA: LifeRhythm.

Leeds, A.M., Shapiro, F. (2000) EMDR and Resource Installation: Principles and Procedures for Enhancing Current Functioning and Resolving Traumatic Experiences. In J. Carlson, & L. Sperry (Ed.), *Brief Therapy Strategies with Individuals and Couples* (Ch. 16, pp. 469–534). Zeig, Tucker, Theisen, Inc, Phoenix, AZ.

Leeds, A. (2001). Principles and Procedures for Enhancing Current Functioning in Complex Posttraumatic Stress Disorder with EMDR Resource Development and Installation. *EMDRIA Newsletter*, Special Edition, pp. 4–11.

Levine, P. (1997). *Waking the Tiger.* Berkeley, CA: North Atlantic Books.

Lipton, B. (2005). *Biology of Belief.* USA: Hay House, Inc.

MacNaughton, I., & Levine, P. (Ed.). (2004). *Body, Breath & Consciousness*. Berkeley, CA: North Atlantic Books.

Marcher, L., & Fich, S. (2010). *Body Encyclopedia: A Guide to the Psychological Functions of the Muscular System*. Berkeley, CA: North Atlantic Books.

Shapiro, F., (2001). *Eye Movement Desensitization and Reprocessing (EMDR): Basic Principles, Protocols, and Procedures*, 2nd Edition. New York, NY: The Guilford Press.

Shapiro, F., (2012) *Getting Past Your Past: Take Control of Your Life with Self-Help Techniques from EMDR Therapy*. New York, NY: Rodale

Siegel, B., (1986) *Love, Medicine & Miracles*. New York, NY: Harper & Row, Publishers, Inc.

Stevens, R., (2007). *Conscious Language™: The Logos of Now*. Asheville, NC: Mastery Systems.

Access Consciousness®. Gary Douglas. accessconsciousness.com

Bodynamic International. Denmark. bodynamic.dk

Bodynamic USA. bodynamicusa.com

Dr. Maarten Klatte. moeiteloosgezond.nl/medische-praktijk/consult

EMDR Research Foundation. http://emdrresearchfoundation.org

Francine Shapiro Library. http://emdria.omeka.net

Lifespan Integration. Peggy Pace. lifespanintegration.com

Neurological Reorganization Therapy. Bette Lamont. neurologicalreorganization.org

TAT® (Tapas Acupressure Technique). Tapas Fleming. tatlife.com

About the Author

Debra Littrell, MA, LMHC is a facilitator, author, speaker, workshop facilitator, consultant, trainer and psychotherapist. She began her career in the mental health field in 1977. She has worked in locked psychiatric settings, crisis centers, juvenile justice, social services, mental health, and private practice. About ten years into her career she began noticing that traditional methods for treatment were not providing change for a significant number of people.

Debra began a journey of asking questions. What would offer change? What prevented change from occurring? What else is available or could be created that would give people the relief they were looking for? She began exploring alternative methods of treatment, some of which became clinically validated in later years. She studied body centered psychotherapies, various spiritual traditions, and a variety of energetic modalities.

She explores with her clients what works for them to design individualized plans. This has meant stepping out of the traditional prescribed-treatment box and into a more fluid way of working. Debra prefers to work as a facilitator of change since the traditional psychotherapy box limits what is possible for change. Especially if insurance is used.

Debra has been on Faculty with the EMDR Institute since 1996. She has provided critical incident services and crisis intervention for emergency service personnel and businesses. She has written a number of training programs for mental health practitioners, teachers, emergency service personnel and the general public. Debra has also been a facilitator for a number of organizations.

She lives and works in Bellevue, WA, USA. She writes, consults, teaches and sees clients both as a facilitator/coach and in psychotherapy. In her free time she enjoys walking, hiking, hanging out with friends and learning new things.

She can be reached at 425-747-5774 or you can visit her website at transformativespirit.com or her retail site at transformativeproductions.com.

Audio Publications

CD & MP3 downloads

Somatic Resourcing 1: Mindfulness & Support Activities
Somatic Resourcing 2: Grounding Exercises

For more information on these go to:

transformativeproductions.com

www.ingramcontent.com/pod-product-compliance
Lightning Source LLC
Chambersburg PA
CBHW071608080526
44588CB00010B/1061